Logic
Course Reader

Younan

ISBN-13: 978-1535513753
ISBN-10: 1535513756

TABLE OF CONTENTS

From Nietzsche, *On Truth and Lie in an Extra-Moral Sense*, tr. Walter Kaufmann:

In some remote corner of the universe, poured out and glittering in innumerable solar systems, there once was a star on which clever animals invented knowledge. That was the highest and most mendacious minute of "world history"—yet only a minute. After nature had drawn a few breaths the star grew cold, and the clever animals had to die.

One might invent such a fable and still not have illustrated sufficiently how wretched, how shadowy and flighty, how aimless and arbitrary, the human intellect appears in nature. There have been eternities when it did not exist; and when it is done for again, nothing will have happened. For this intellect has no further mission that would lead beyond human life. It is human, rather, and only its owner and producer gives it such importance, as if the world pivoted around it. But if we could communicate with the mosquito, then we would learn that he floats through the air with the same self-importance, feeling within itself the flying center of the world. There is nothing in nature so despicable or insignificant that it cannot immediately be blown up like a bag by a slight breath of this power of knowledge; and just as every porter wants an admirer, the proudest human being, the philosopher, thinks that he sees on the eyes of the universe telescopically focused from all sides on his actions and thoughts.

It is strange that this should be the effect of the intellect, for after all it was given only as an aid to the most unfortunate, most delicate, most evanescent beings in order to hold them for a minute in existence, from which otherwise, without this gift, they would have every reason to flee as quickly as Lessing's son. [In a famous letter to Johann

1

Joachim Eschenburg (December 31, 1778), Lessing relates the death of his infant son, who "understood the world so well that he left it at the first opportunity."] That haughtiness which goes with knowledge and feeling, which shrouds the eyes and senses of man in a blinding fog, therefore deceives him about the value of existence by carrying in itself the most flattering evaluation of knowledge itself. Its most universal effect is deception; but even its most particular effects have something of the same character.

The intellect, as a means for the preservation of the individual, unfolds its chief powers in simulation; for this is the means by which the weaker, less robust individuals preserve themselves, since they are denied the chance of waging the struggle for existence with horns or the fangs of beasts of prey. In man this art of simulation reaches its peak: here deception, flattering, lying and cheating, talking behind the back, posing, living in borrowed splendor, being masked, the disguise of convention, acting a role before others and before oneself—in short, the constant fluttering around the single flame of vanity is so much the rule and the law that almost nothing is more incomprehensible than how an honest and pure urge for truth could make its appearance among men. They are deeply immersed in illusions and dream images; their eye glides only over the surface of things and sees "forms"; their feeling nowhere lead into truth, but contents itself with the reception of stimuli, playing, as it were, a game of blindman's buff on the backs of things. Moreover, man permits himself to be lied to at night, his life long, when he dreams, and his moral sense never even tries to prevent this—although men have been said to have overcome snoring by sheer will power.

What, indeed, does man know of himself! Can he even once perceive himself completely, laid out as if in an illuminated glass case? Does not nature keep much the most from him, even about his body, to spellbind and confine him in a proud, deceptive consciousness, far from the coils of the intestines, the quick current of the blood stream, and the involved tremors of the fibers? She threw away the key; and woe to the calamitous curiosity which might peer just once through a crack in the chamber of consciousness and look down, and sense that man rests upon the merciless, the greedy, the insatiable, the murderous, in the indifference of his ignorance—hanging in dreams, as it were, upon the back of a tiger. In view of this, whence in all the world comes the urge for truth?

Insofar as the individual wants to preserve himself against other individuals, in a natural state of affairs he employs the intellect mostly for simulation alone. But because man, out of need and boredom, wants to exist socially, herd-fashion, he requires a peace pact and he endeavors to banish at least the very crudest *bellum omni contra omnes* [war of all against all] from his world. This peace pact brings with it something that looks like the first step toward the attainment of this enigmatic urge for truth. For now that is fixed which henceforth shall be "truth"; that is, a regularly valid and obligatory designation of things is invented, and this linguistic legislation also furnishes the first laws of truth: for it is here that the contrast between truth and lie first originates. The liar uses the valid designations, the words, to make the unreal appear as real; he says, for example, "I am rich," when the word "poor" would be the correct designation of his situation. He abuses the fixed conventions by arbitrary changes or even by reversals of the names. When he does this in a self-serving way damaging to others, then society will no longer trust him but exclude him. Thereby men do not flee from being deceived as much as from being damaged by deception: what they hate at this stage is basically not the deception but the bad, hostile consequences of certain kinds of deceptions. In a similarly limited way man wants the truth: he desires the agreeable life-preserving consequences of truth, but he is indifferent to pure knowledge, which has no consequences; he is even hostile to possibly damaging and destructive truths. And, moreover, what about these conventions of language? Are they really the products of knowledge, of the sense of truth? Do the designations and the things coincide? Is language the adequate expression of all realities?

Only through forgetfulness can man ever achieve the illusion of possessing a "truth" in the sense just designated. If he does not wish to be satisfied with truth in the form of a tautology—that is, with empty shells—then he will forever buy illusions for truths. What is a word? The image of a nerve stimulus in sounds. But to infer from the nerve stimulus, a cause outside us, that is already the result of a false and unjustified application of the principle of reason...The different languages, set side by side, show that what matters with words is never the truth, never an adequate expression; else there would not be so many languages. The "thing in itself" (for that is what pure truth, without consequences, would be) is quite incomprehensible to the creators of language and not at all worth aiming for. One designates only the relations of things to man, and to express them one calls on the boldest metaphors. A nerve stimulus, first transposed into an image—first metaphor. The image, in turn, imitated by a sound—second metaphor...

Let us still give special consideration to the formation of concepts. Every word immediately becomes a concept, inasmuch as it is not intended to serve as a reminder of the unique and wholly individualized original experience to which it owes its birth, but must at the same time fit innumerable, more or less similar cases—which means, strictly speaking, never equal—in other words, a lot of unequal cases. Every concept originates through our equating what is unequal. No leaf ever wholly equals another, and the concept "leaf" is formed through an arbitrary abstraction from these individual differences, through forgetting the distinctions; and now it gives rise to the idea that in nature there might be something besides the leaves which would be "leaf"—some kind of original form after which all leaves have been woven, marked, copied, colored, curled, and painted, but by unskilled hands, so that no copy turned out to be a correct, reliable, and faithful image of the original form. We call a person "honest." Why did he act so honestly today? we ask. Our answer usually sounds like this: because of his honesty. Honesty! That is to say again: the leaf is the cause of the leaves. After all, we know nothing of an essence-like quality named "honesty"; we know only numerous individualized, and thus unequal actions, which we equate by omitting the unequal and by then calling them honest actions. In the end, we distill from them a *qualitas occulta* [hidden quality] with the name of "honesty"...

What, then, is truth? A mobile army of metaphors, metonyms, and anthropomorphisms—in short, a sum of human relations which have been enhanced, transposed, and embellished poetically and rhetorically, and which after long use seem firm, canonical, and obligatory to a people: truths are illusions about which one has forgotten that this is what they are; metaphors which are worn out and without sensuous power; coins which have lost their pictures and now matter only as metal, no longer as coins.

5

We still do not know where the urge for truth comes from; for as yet we have heard only of the obligation imposed by society that it should exist: to be truthful means using the customary metaphors—in moral terms: the obligation to lie according to a fixed convention, to lie herd-like in a style obligatory for all...

From Plato's *Phaedo*, tr. Benjamin Jowett:

All of us, as we afterwards remarked to one another, had an unpleasant feeling at hearing what they said. When we had been so firmly convinced before, now to have our faith shaken seemed to introduce a confusion and uncertainty, not only into the previous argument, but into any future one; either we were incapable of forming a judgment, or there were no grounds of belief.

ECHECRATES: There I feel with you--by heaven I do, Phaedo, and when you were speaking, I was beginning to ask myself the same question: What argument can I ever trust again? For what could be more convincing than the argument of Socrates, which has now fallen into discredit? That the soul is a harmony is a doctrine which has always had a wonderful attraction for me, and, when mentioned, came back to me at once, as my own original conviction. And now I must begin again and find another argument which will assure me that when the man is dead the soul survives. Tell me, I implore you, how did Socrates proceed? Did he appear to share the unpleasant feeling which you mention? or did he calmly meet the attack? And did he answer forcibly or feebly? Narrate what passed as exactly as you can.

PHAEDO: Often, Echecrates, I have wondered at Socrates, but never more than on that occasion. That he should be able to answer was nothing, but what astonished me was, first, the gentle and pleasant and approving manner in which he received the words of the young men, and then his quick sense of the wound which had been inflicted by the argument, and the readiness with which he healed it. He might be compared to a general rallying his defeated and broken army, urging them to accompany him and return to the field of argument.

ECHECRATES: What followed?

PHAEDO: You shall hear, for I was close to him on his right hand, seated on a sort of stool, and he on a couch which was a good deal higher. He stroked my head, and pressed the hair upon my neck--he had a way of playing with my hair; and then he said: To-morrow, Phaedo, I suppose that these fair locks of yours will be severed.

Yes, Socrates, I suppose that they will, I replied.

Not so, if you will take my advice.

What shall I do with them? I said.

To-day, he replied, and not to-morrow, if this argument dies and we cannot bring it to life again, you and I will both shave our locks; and if I were you, and the argument got away from me, and I could not hold my ground against Simmias and Cebes, I would myself take an oath, like the Argives, not to wear hair any more until I had renewed the conflict and defeated them.

Yes, I said, but Heracles himself is said not to be a match for two.

Summon me then, he said, and I will be your Iolaus until the sun goes down.

I summon you rather, I rejoined, not as Heracles summoning Iolaus, but as Iolaus might summon Heracles.

That will do as well, he said. But first let us take care that we avoid a danger.

Of what nature? I said.

Lest we become misologists, he replied, no worse thing can happen to a man than this. For as there are misanthropists or haters of men, there are also misologists or haters of ideas, and both spring from the same cause, which is ignorance of the world. Misanthropy arises out of the too great confidence of inexperience;--you trust a man and think him altogether true and sound and faithful, and then in a little while he turns out to be false and knavish; and then another and another, and when this has happened several times to a man, especially when it happens among those whom he deems to be his own most trusted and familiar friends, and he has often quarreled with them, he at last hates all men, and believes that no one has any good in him at all. You must have observed this trait of character?

I have.

And is not the feeling discreditable? Is it not obvious that such an one having to deal with other men, was clearly without any experience of human nature; for experience would have taught him the true state of the case, that few are the good and few the evil, and that the great majority are in the interval between them.

What do you mean? I said.

I mean, he replied, as you might say of the very large and very small, that nothing is more uncommon than a very large or very small man; and this applies generally to all extremes, whether of great and small, or swift and slow, or fair and foul, or black and white: and whether the instances you select be men or dogs or anything else, few are the extremes, but many are in the mean between them. Did you never observe this?

Yes, I said, I have.

And do you not imagine, he said, that if there were a competition in evil, the worst would be found to be very few?

Yes, that is very likely, I said.

Yes, that is very likely, he replied; although in this respect arguments are unlike men--there I was led on by you to say more than I had intended; but the point of comparison was, that when a simple man who has no skill in dialectics believes an argument to be true which he afterwards imagines to be false, whether really false or not, and then another and another, he has no longer any faith left, and great disputers, as you know, come to think at last that they have grown to be the wisest of mankind; for they alone perceive the utter unsoundness and instability of all arguments, or indeed, of all things, which, like the currents in the Euripus, are going up and down in never-ceasing ebb and flow.

That is quite true, I said.

Yes, Phaedo, he replied, and how melancholy, if there be such a thing as truth or certainty or possibility of knowledge--that a man should have lighted upon some argument or other which at first seemed true and then turned out to be false, and instead of blaming himself and his own want of wit, because he is annoyed, should at last be too glad to transfer the blame from himself to arguments in general: and forever afterwards should hate and revile them, and lose truth and the knowledge of realities.

Yes, indeed, I said; that is very melancholy.

Let us then, in the first place, he said, be careful of allowing or of admitting into our souls the notion that there is no health or soundness in any arguments at all. Rather say that we have not yet attained to soundness in ourselves, and that we must struggle manfully and do our best to gain health of mind--you and all other men having regard to the whole of your future life, and I myself in the prospect of death. For at this moment I am sensible that I have not the temper of a philosopher; like the vulgar, I am only a partisan. Now the partisan, when he is engaged in a dispute, cares nothing about the rights of the question, but is anxious only to convince his hearers of his own assertions. And the difference between him and me at the present moment is merely this--that whereas he seeks to convince his hearers that what he says is true, I am rather seeking to convince myself; to convince my hearers is a secondary matter with me. And do but see how much I gain by the argument. For if what I say is true, then I do well to be persuaded of the truth, but if there be nothing after death, still, during the short time that remains, I shall not distress my friends with lamentations, and my ignorance will not last, but will die with me, and therefore no harm will be done. This is the state of mind, Simmias and Cebes, in which I approach the argument. And I would ask you to be thinking of the truth and not of Socrates: agree with me, if I seem to you to be speaking the truth; or if not, withstand me might and main, that I may not deceive you as well as myself in my enthusiasm, and like the bee, leave my sting in you before I die:

From St. Thomas Aquinas, *Commentary on the Posterior Analytics*, Preface:

As the Philosopher says in *Metaphysics* I (980b26), "the human race lives by art and reasonings." In this statement the Philosopher seems to touch upon that property whereby man differs from the other animals. For the other animals are prompted to their acts by a natural impulse, but man is directed in his actions by a judgment of reason. And this is the reason why there are various arts devoted to the ready and orderly performance of human acts. For an art seems to be nothing more than a definite and fixed procedure established by reason, whereby human acts reach their due end through appropriate means.

Now reason is not only able to direct the acts of the lower powers but is also the director of its own act: for what is peculiar to the intellective part of man is its ability to reflect upon itself. For the intellect knows itself. In like manner reason is able to reason about its own act. Therefore just as the art of building or carpentering, through which man is enabled to perform manual acts in an easy and orderly manner, arose from the fact that reason reasoned about manual acts, so in like manner an art is needed to direct the act of reasoning, so that by it a man when performing the act of reasoning might proceed in an orderly and easy manner and without error. And this art is logic, i.e., the science of reason. And it concerns reason not only because it is according to reason, for that is common to all arts, but also because it is concerned with the very act of reasoning as with its proper matter. Therefore it seems to be the art of arts, because it directs us in the act of reasoning, from which all arts proceed. Consequently one should view the parts of logic according to the diversity among the acts of reason.

Now there are three acts of reason, the first two of which belong to reason regarded as intellect. One action of the intellect is the understanding of indivisible or uncomplex things, and according to this action it conceives *what* a thing is. And this operation is called by some the informing of the intellect, or representing by means of the intellect. To this operation of the reason is ordained the doctrine which Aristotle hands down in the book of *Predicaments* (i.e., the Categories). The second operation of the intellect is its act of combining or dividing, in which the true or the false are for the first time present. And this act of reason is the subject of the doctrine which Aristotle hands down in the book entitled *On Interpretation*. But the third act of the reason is concerned with that which is peculiar to reason, namely, to advance from one thing to another in such a way that through that which is known a man comes to a knowledge of the unknown. And this act is considered in the remaining books of logic.

THE THREE ACTS OF THE INTELLECT

Act of Intellect	Focus	Product	Characteristics	Question
1. Simple Apprehension *(abstracts from senses)*	Essences or Natures	Concept/ Term	Clear or Unclear	What?
2. Judgment *(unites 2 concepts)*	Acts of Existence - "is"	Proposition	True or False	Whether?
3. Reasoning *(makes a conclusion)*	Causes or Reasons	Argument	Valid or Invalid	Why?

SIMPLE APPREHENSION - TEXTS

Aristotle, *Categories*, tr. E. M. Edghill

Section 1

Part 1

[handwritten: ambiguous]

Things are said to be named ('equivocally') when, though they have a common name, the (definition) corresponding with the name (differs) for each. Thus, a real man and a figure in a picture can both lay claim to the name 'animal'; yet these are equivocally so named, for, though they have a common name, the definition corresponding with the name differs for each. For should any one define in what sense each is an animal, his definition in the one case will be appropriate to that case only.

[handwritten: having one meaning or unambiguous]

On the other hand, things are said to be named ('univocally') which have both the name and the (definition) answering to the name in (common) A man and an ox are both 'animal', and these are univocally so named, inasmuch as not only the name, but also the definition, is the same in both cases: for if a man should state in what sense each is an animal, the statement in the one case would be identical with that in the other.

Things are said to be named 'derivatively', which derive their name from some other name, but (differ) from it in (termination) Thus the grammarian derives his name from the word 'grammar', and the courageous man from the word 'courage'.

[handwritten: grammarian & grammer have two different definitions but stem from similar name]

15

Part 2

composed of
made up not
separate parts

Forms of speech are either simple or (composite.) Examples of
the latter are such expressions as 'the man runs', 'the man
wins'; of the former 'man', 'ox', 'runs', 'wins'.

affirmed → *Said of*

Of things themselves some are (predicable) of a subject, and
are never present in a subject. [Thus 'man' is predicable of the
individual man, and is never present in a subject.] ?

[By being 'present in a subject' I do not mean present as parts
are present in a whole, but being incapable of existence apart
from the said subject.] ?

*How
does
this
apply?*

Some things, again, are present in a subject, but are never
predicable of a subject. For instance, a certain point of
grammatical knowledge is present in the mind, but is not
predicable of any subject; or again, a certain whiteness may
be present in the body (for colour requires a material basis),
yet it is never predicable of anything. *Significance?*

Other things, again, are both predicable of a subject and
present in a subject. [Thus while knowledge is present in the
human mind, it is predicable of grammar.] ?

?

There is, lastly, a class of things which are neither present in
a subject nor predicable of a subject, such as the individual
man or the individual horse. But, to speak more generally,
that which is individual and has the character of a unit is
never predicable of a subject. Yet in some cases there is
nothing to prevent such being present in a subject. Thus a
certain point of grammatical knowledge is present in a
subject.

Part 3

When one thing is predicated of another, all that which is predicable of the predicate will be predicable also of the subject. Thus, 'man' is predicated of the individual man; but 'animal' is predicated of 'man'; it will, therefore, be predicable of the individual man also: for the individual man is both 'man' and 'animal'.

If genera are different and co-ordinate, their differentiae are themselves different in kind. Take as an instance the genus 'animal' and the genus 'knowledge'. 'With feet', 'two-footed', 'winged', 'aquatic', are differentiae of 'animal'; the species of knowledge are not distinguished by the same differentiae. One species of knowledge does not differ from another in being 'two-footed'.

But where one genus is subordinate to another, there is nothing to prevent their having the same differentiae: for the greater class is predicated of the lesser, so that all the differentiae of the predicate will be differentiae also of the subject.

Part 4

Expressions which are in no way composite signify substance, quantity, quality, relation, place, time, position, state, action, or affection. To sketch my meaning roughly, examples of substance are 'man' or 'the horse', of quantity, such terms as 'two cubits long' or 'three cubits long', of quality, such attributes as 'white', 'grammatical'. 'Double', 'half', 'greater', fall under the category of relation; 'in the market place', 'in the Lyceum', under that of place;

'yesterday', 'last year', under that of time. 'Lying', 'sitting', are terms indicating position, 'shod', 'armed', state; 'to lance', 'to cauterize', action; 'to be lanced', 'to be cauterized', affection.

No one of these terms, in and by itself, involves an affirmation; it is by the combination of such terms that positive or negative statements arise. For every assertion must, as is admitted, be either true or false, whereas expressions which are not in any way composite such as 'man', 'white', 'runs', 'wins', cannot be either true or false.

Part 5

Substance, in the truest and primary and most definite sense of the word, is that which is neither predicable of a subject nor present in a subject; for instance, the individual man or horse. But in a secondary sense those things are called substances within which, as species, the primary substances are included; also those which, as genera, include the species. For instance, the individual man is included in the species 'man', and the genus to which the species belongs is 'animal'; these, therefore—that is to say, the species 'man' and the genus 'animal,-are termed secondary substances.

It is plain from what has been said that both the name and the definition of the predicate must be predicable of the subject. For instance, 'man' is predicated of the individual man. Now in this case the name of the species 'man' is applied to the individual, for we use the term 'man' in describing the individual; and the definition of 'man' will also be predicated of the individual man, for the individual man is both man and animal. Thus, both the name and the definition of the species are predicable of the individual.

With regard, on the other hand, to those things which are present in a subject, it is generally the case that neither their name nor their definition is predicable of that in which they are present. Though, however, the definition is never predicable, there is nothing in certain cases to prevent the name being used. For instance, 'white' being present in a body is predicated of that in which it is present, for a body is called white: the definition, however, of the colour 'white' is never predicable of the body.

Everything except primary substances is either predicable of a primary substance or present in a primary substance. This becomes evident by reference to particular instances which occur. 'Animal' is predicated of the species 'man', therefore of the individual man, for if there were no individual man of whom it could be predicated, it could not be predicated of the species 'man' at all. Again, colour is present in body, therefore in individual bodies, for if there were no individual body in which it was present, it could not be present in body at all. Thus everything except primary substances is either predicated of primary substances, or is present in them, and if these last did not exist, it would be impossible for anything else to exist.

Of secondary substances, the species is more truly substance than the genus, being more nearly related to primary substance. For if any one should render an account of what a primary substance is, he would render a more instructive account, and one more proper to the subject, by stating the species than by stating the genus. Thus, he would give a more instructive account of an individual man by stating that he was man than by stating that he was animal, for the former description is peculiar to the individual in a greater degree, while the latter is too general. Again, the man who gives an account of the nature of an individual tree will give a more instructive account by mentioning the species 'tree' than by mentioning the genus 'plant'.

Moreover, primary substances are most properly called substances in virtue of the fact that they are the entities which underlie everything else, and that everything else is either predicated of them or present in them. Now the same relation which subsists between primary substance and everything else subsists also between the species and the genus: for the species is to the genus as subject is to predicate, since the genus is predicated of the species, whereas the species cannot be predicated of the genus. Thus we have a second ground for asserting that the species is more truly substance than the genus.

Of species themselves, except in the case of such as are genera, no one is more truly substance than another. We should not give a more appropriate account of the individual man by stating the species to which he belonged, than we should of an individual horse by adopting the same method of definition. In the same way, of primary substances, no one is more truly substance than another; an individual man is not more truly substance than an individual ox.

It is, then, with good reason that of all that remains, when we exclude primary substances, we concede to species and genera alone the name 'secondary substance', for these alone of all the predicates convey a knowledge of primary substance. For it is by stating the species or the genus that we appropriately define any individual man; and we shall make our definition more exact by stating the former than by stating the latter. All other things that we state, such as that he is white, that he runs, and so on, are irrelevant to the definition. Thus it is just that these alone, apart from primary substances, should be called substances.

Further, primary substances are most properly so called, because they underlie and are the subjects of everything else. Now the same relation that subsists between primary substance and everything else subsists also between the species and the genus to which the primary substance belongs, on the one hand, and every attribute which is not included within these, on the other. For these are the subjects of all such. If we call an individual man 'skilled in grammar', the predicate is applicable also to the species and to the genus to which he belongs. This law holds good in all cases.

It is a common characteristic of all substance that it is never present in a subject. For primary substance is neither present in a subject nor predicated of a subject; while, with regard to secondary substances, it is clear from the following arguments (apart from others) that they are not present in a subject. For 'man' is predicated of the individual man, but is not present in any subject: for manhood is not present in the individual man. In the same way, 'animal' is also predicated of the individual man, but is not present in him. Again, when a thing is present in a subject, though the name may quite well be applied to that in which it is present, the definition cannot be applied. Yet of secondary substances, not only the name, but also the definition, applies to the subject: we should use both the definition of the species and that of the genus with reference to the individual man. Thus substance cannot be present in a subject.

Yet this is not peculiar to substance, for it is also the case that differentiae cannot be present in subjects. The characteristics 'terrestrial' and 'two-footed' are predicated of the species 'man', but not present in it. For they are not in man. Moreover, the definition of the differentia may be predicated of that of which the differentia itself is predicated. For instance, if the characteristic 'terrestrial' is predicated of the species 'man', the definition also of that characteristic may be used to form the predicate of the species 'man': for 'man' is terrestrial.

The fact that the parts of substances appear to be present in the whole, as in a subject, should not make us apprehensive lest we should have to admit that such parts are not substances: for in explaining the phrase 'being present in a subject', we stated' that we meant 'otherwise than as parts in a whole'.

It is the mark of substances and of differentiae that, in all propositions of which they form the predicate, they are predicated univocally. For all such propositions have for their subject either the individual or the species. It is true that, inasmuch as primary substance is not predicable of anything, it can never form the predicate of any proposition. But of secondary substances, the species is predicated of the individual, the genus both of the species and of the individual. Similarly the differentiae are predicated of the species and of the individuals. Moreover, the definition of the species and that of the genus are applicable to the primary substance, and that of the genus to the species. For all that is predicated of the predicate will be predicated also of the subject. Similarly, the definition of the differentiae will be applicable to the species and to the individuals. But it was stated above that the word 'univocal' was applied to those things which had both name and definition in common. It is, therefore, established that in every proposition, of which either substance or a differentia forms the predicate, these are predicated univocally.

All substance appears to signify that which is individual. In the case of primary substance this is indisputably true, for the thing is a unit. In the case of secondary substances, when we speak, for instance, of 'man' or 'animal', our form of speech gives the impression that we are here also indicating that which is individual, but the impression is not strictly true; for a secondary substance is not an individual, but a class with a certain qualification; for it is not one and single as a primary substance is; the words 'man', 'animal', are predicable of more than one subject.

Yet species and genus do not merely indicate quality, like the term 'white'; 'white' indicates quality and nothing further, but species and genus determine the quality with reference to a substance: they signify substance qualitatively differentiated. The determinate qualification covers a larger field in the case of the genus that in that of the species: he who uses the word 'animal' is herein using a word of wider extension than he who uses the word 'man'.

Another mark of substance is that it has no contrary. What could be the contrary of any primary substance, such as the individual man or animal? It has none. Nor can the species or the genus have a contrary. Yet this characteristic is not peculiar to substance, but is true of many other things, such as quantity. There is nothing that forms the contrary of 'two cubits long' or of 'three cubits long', or of 'ten', or of any such term. A man may contend that 'much' is the contrary of 'little', or 'great' of 'small', but of definite quantitative terms no contrary exists.

Substance, again, does not appear to admit of variation of degree. I do not mean by this that one substance cannot be more or less truly substance than another, for it has already been stated that this is the case; but that no single substance admits of varying degrees within itself. For instance, one particular substance, 'man', cannot be more or less man either than himself at some other time or than some other man. One man cannot be more man than another, as that which is white may be more or less white than some other white object, or as that which is beautiful may be more or less beautiful than some other beautiful object. The same quality, moreover, is said to subsist in a thing in varying degrees at different times. A body, being white, is said to be whiter at one time than it was before, or, being warm, is said to be warmer or less warm than at some other time. But substance is not said to be more or less that which it is: a man is not more truly a man at one time than he was before, nor is anything, if it is substance, more or less what it is. Substance, then, does not admit of variation of degree.

The most distinctive mark of substance appears to be that, while remaining numerically one and the same, it is capable of admitting contrary qualities. From among things other than substance, we should find ourselves unable to bring forward any which possessed this mark. Thus, one and the same colour cannot be white and black. Nor can the same one action be good and bad: this law holds good with everything that is not substance. But one and the selfsame substance, while retaining its identity, is yet capable of admitting contrary qualities. The same individual person is at one time white, at another black, at one time warm, at another cold, at one time good, at another bad. This capacity is found nowhere else, though it might be maintained that a statement or opinion was an exception to the rule. The same statement, it is agreed, can be both true and false. For if the statement 'he is sitting' is true, yet, when the person in question has risen, the same statement will be false. The same applies to opinions. For if any one thinks truly that a person is sitting, yet, when that person has risen, this same opinion, if still held, will be false. Yet although this exception may be allowed, there is, nevertheless, a difference in the manner in which the thing takes place. It is by themselves changing that substances admit contrary qualities. It is thus that that which was hot becomes cold, for it has entered into a different state. Similarly that which was white becomes black, and that which was bad good, by a process of change; and in the same way in all other cases it is by changing that substances are capable of admitting contrary qualities. But statements and opinions themselves remain unaltered in all respects: it is by the alteration in the facts of the case that the contrary quality comes to be theirs. The statement 'he is sitting' remains unaltered, but it is at one time true, at another false, according to circumstances. What has been said of statements applies also to opinions. Thus, in respect of the manner in which the thing takes place, it is the peculiar mark of substance that it should be capable of admitting contrary qualities; for it is by itself changing that it does so.

If, then, a man should make this exception and contend that statements and opinions are capable of admitting contrary qualities, his contention is unsound. For statements and opinions are said to have this capacity, not because they themselves undergo modification, but because this modification occurs in the case of something else. The truth or falsity of a statement depends on facts, and not on any power on the part of the statement itself of admitting contrary qualities. In short, there is nothing which can alter the nature of statements and opinions. As, then, no change takes place in themselves, these cannot be said to be capable of admitting contrary qualities.

But it is by reason of the modification which takes place within the substance itself that a substance is said to be capable of admitting contrary qualities; for a substance admits within itself either disease or health, whiteness or blackness. It is in this sense that it is said to be capable of admitting contrary qualities.

To sum up, it is a distinctive mark of substance, that, while remaining numerically one and the same, it is capable of admitting contrary qualities, the modification taking place through a change in the substance itself.

Let these remarks suffice on the subject of substance.

Part 6

Quantity is either discrete or continuous. Moreover, some quantities are such that each part of the whole has a relative position to the other parts: others have within them no such relation of part to part.

Instances of discrete quantities are number and speech; of continuous, lines, surfaces, solids, and, besides these, time and place.

In the case of the parts of a number, there is no common boundary at which they join. For example: two fives make ten, but the two fives have no common boundary, but are separate; the parts three and seven also do not join at any boundary. Nor, to generalize, would it ever be possible in the case of number that there should be a common boundary among the parts; they are always separate. Number, therefore, is a discrete quantity.

The same is true of speech. That speech is a quantity is evident: for it is measured in long and short syllables. I mean here that speech which is vocal. Moreover, it is a discrete quantity for its parts have no common boundary. There is no common boundary at which the syllables join, but each is separate and distinct from the rest.

A line, on the other hand, is a continuous quantity, for it is possible to find a common boundary at which its parts join. In the case of the line, this common boundary is the point; in the case of the plane, it is the line: for the parts of the plane have also a common boundary. Similarly you can find a common boundary in the case of the parts of a solid, namely either a line or a plane.

Space and time also belong to this class of quantities. Time, past, present, and future, forms a continuous whole. Space, likewise, is a continuous quantity; for the parts of a solid occupy a certain space, and these have a common boundary; it follows that the parts of space also, which are occupied by

27

the parts of the solid, have the same common boundary as the parts of the solid. Thus, not only time, but space also, is a continuous quantity, for its parts have a common boundary.

Quantities consist either of parts which bear a relative position each to each, or of parts which do not. The parts of a line bear a relative position to each other, for each lies somewhere, and it would be possible to distinguish each, and to state the position of each on the plane and to explain to what sort of part among the rest each was contiguous. Similarly the parts of a plane have position, for it could similarly be stated what was the position of each and what sort of parts were contiguous. The same is true with regard to the solid and to space. But it would be impossible to show that the parts of a number had a relative position each to each, or a particular position, or to state what parts were contiguous. Nor could this be done in the case of time, for none of the parts of time has an abiding existence, and that which does not abide can hardly have position. It would be better to say that such parts had a relative order, in virtue of one being prior to another. Similarly with number: in counting, 'one' is prior to 'two', and 'two' to 'three', and thus the parts of number may be said to possess a relative order, though it would be impossible to discover any distinct position for each. This holds good also in the case of speech. None of its parts has an abiding existence: when once a syllable is pronounced, it is not possible to retain it, so that, naturally, as the parts do not abide, they cannot have position. Thus, some quantities consist of parts which have position, and some of those which have not.

Strictly speaking, only the things which I have mentioned belong to the category of quantity: everything else that is called quantitative is a quantity in a secondary sense. It is because we have in mind some one of these quantities, properly so called, that we apply quantitative terms to other things. We speak of what is white as large, because the surface over which the white extends is large; we speak of an action or a process as lengthy, because the time covered is long; these things cannot in their own right claim the quantitative epithet. For instance, should any one explain how long an action was, his statement would be made in terms of the time taken, to the effect that it lasted a year, or something of that sort. In the same way, he would explain the size of a white object in terms of surface, for he would state the area which it covered. Thus the things already mentioned, and these alone, are in their intrinsic nature quantities; nothing else can claim the name in its own right, but, if at all, only in a secondary sense.

Quantities have no contraries. In the case of definite quantities this is obvious; thus, there is nothing that is the contrary of 'two cubits long' or of 'three cubits long', or of a surface, or of any such quantities. A man might, indeed, argue that 'much' was the contrary of 'little', and 'great' of 'small'. But these are not quantitative, but relative; things are not great or small absolutely, they are so called rather as the result of an act of comparison. For instance, a mountain is called small, a grain large, in virtue of the fact that the latter is greater than others of its kind, the former less. Thus there is a reference here to an external standard, for if the terms 'great' and 'small' were used absolutely, a mountain would never be called small or a grain large. Again, we say that there are many people in a village, and few in Athens, although those in the city are many times as numerous as those in the village: or we say that a house has many in it, and a theatre few, though those in the theatre far outnumber those in the house. The terms 'two cubits long', 'three cubits long', and so on indicate quantity, the terms 'great' and 'small' indicate relation, for they have reference to an external standard. It is, therefore, plain that these are to be classed as relative.

Again, whether we define them as quantitative or not, they have no contraries: for how can there be a contrary of an attribute which is not to be apprehended in or by itself, but only by reference to something external? Again, if 'great' and 'small' are contraries, it will come about that the same subject can admit contrary qualities at one and the same time, and that things will themselves be contrary to themselves. For it happens at times that the same thing is both small and great. For the same thing may be small in comparison with one thing, and great in comparison with another, so that the same thing comes to be both small and great at one and the same time, and is of such a nature as to admit contrary qualities at one and the same moment. Yet it was agreed, when substance was being discussed, that nothing admits contrary qualities at one and the same moment. For though substance is capable of admitting contrary qualities, yet no one is at the same time both sick and healthy, nothing is at the same time both white and black. Nor is there anything which is qualified in contrary ways at one and the same time.

Moreover, if these were contraries, they would themselves be contrary to themselves. For if 'great' is the contrary of 'small', and the same thing is both great and small at the same time, then 'small' or 'great' is the contrary of itself. But this is impossible. The term 'great', therefore, is not the contrary of the term 'small', nor 'much' of 'little'. And even though a man should call these terms not relative but quantitative, they would not have contraries.

It is in the case of space that quantity most plausibly appears to admit of a contrary. For men define the term 'above' as the contrary of 'below', when it is the region at the centre they mean by 'below'; and this is so, because nothing is farther from the extremities of the universe than the region at the centre. Indeed, it seems that in defining contraries of every kind men have recourse to a spatial metaphor, for they say that those things are contraries which, within the same class, are separated by the greatest possible distance.

Quantity does not, it appears, admit of variation of degree. One thing cannot be two cubits long in a greater degree than another. Similarly with regard to number: what is 'three' is not more truly three than what is 'five' is five; nor is one set of three more truly three than another set. Again, one period of time is not said to be more truly time than another. Nor is there any other kind of quantity, of all that have been mentioned, with regard to which variation of degree can be predicated. The category of quantity, therefore, does not admit of variation of degree.

The most distinctive mark of quantity is that equality and inequality are predicated of it. Each of the aforesaid quantities is said to be equal or unequal. For instance, one solid is said to be equal or unequal to another; number, too, and time can have these terms applied to them, indeed can all those kinds of quantity that have been mentioned.

That which is not a quantity can by no means, it would seem, be termed equal or unequal to anything else. One particular disposition or one particular quality, such as whiteness, is by no means compared with another in terms of equality and inequality but rather in terms of similarity. Thus it is the distinctive mark of quantity that it can be called equal and unequal.

Section 2

Part 7

Those things are called relative, which, being either said to be of something else or related to something else, are explained by reference to that other thing. For instance, the word 'superior' is explained by reference to something else, for it is superiority over something else that is meant. Similarly, the expression 'double' has this external reference, for it is the double of something else that is meant. So it is with everything else of this kind. There are, moreover, other relatives, e.g. habit, disposition, perception, knowledge, and attitude. The significance of all these is explained by a reference to something else and in no other way. Thus, a habit is a habit of something, knowledge is knowledge of something, attitude is the attitude of something. So it is with all other relatives that have been mentioned. Those terms, then, are called relative, the nature of which is explained by reference to something else, the preposition 'of' or some other preposition being used to indicate the relation. Thus, one mountain is called great in comparison with another; for the mountain claims this attribute by comparison with something. Again, that which is called similar must be similar to something else, and all other such attributes have this external reference. It is to be noted that lying and standing and sitting are particular attitudes, but attitude is itself a relative term. To lie, to stand, to be seated, are not themselves attitudes, but take their name from the aforesaid attitudes.

It is possible for relatives to have contraries. Thus virtue has a contrary, vice, these both being relatives; knowledge, too, has a contrary, ignorance. But this is not the mark of all relatives; 'double' and 'triple' have no contrary, nor indeed has any such term.

It also appears that relatives can admit of variation of degree. For 'like' and 'unlike', 'equal' and 'unequal', have the modifications 'more' and 'less' applied to them, and each of these is relative in character: for the terms 'like' and 'unequal' bear a reference to something external. Yet, again, it is not every relative term that admits of variation of degree. No term such as 'double' admits of this modification. All relatives have correlatives: by the term 'slave' we mean the slave of a master, by the term 'master', the master of a slave; by 'double', the double of its half; by 'half', the half of its double; by 'greater', greater than that which is less; by 'less', less than that which is greater.

So it is with every other relative term; but the case we use to express the correlation differs in some instances. Thus, by knowledge we mean knowledge of the knowable; by the knowable, that which is to be apprehended by knowledge; by perception, perception of the perceptible; by the perceptible, that which is apprehended by perception.

Sometimes, however, reciprocity of correlation does not appear to exist. This comes about when a blunder is made, and that to which the relative is related is not accurately stated. If a man states that a wing is necessarily relative to a bird, the connexion between these two will not be reciprocal, for it will not be possible to say that a bird is a bird by reason of its wings. The reason is that the original statement was inaccurate, for the wing is not said to be relative to the bird qua bird, since many creatures besides birds have wings, but qua winged creature. If, then, the statement is made accurate, the connexion will be reciprocal, for we can speak of a wing, having reference necessarily to a winged creature, and of a winged creature as being such because of its wings.

Occasionally, perhaps, it is necessary to coin words, if no word exists by which a correlation can adequately be explained. If we define a rudder as necessarily having reference to a boat, our definition will not be appropriate, for the rudder does not have this reference to a boat qua boat, as there are boats which have no rudders. Thus we cannot use the terms reciprocally, for the word 'boat' cannot be said to find its explanation in the word 'rudder'. As there is no existing word, our definition would perhaps be more accurate if we coined some word like 'ruddered' as the correlative of 'rudder'. If we express ourselves thus accurately, at any rate the terms are reciprocally connected, for the 'ruddered' thing is 'ruddered' in virtue of its rudder. So it is in all other cases. A head will be more accurately defined as the correlative of that which is 'headed', than as that of an animal, for the animal does not have a head qua animal, since many animals have no head.

Thus we may perhaps most easily comprehend that to which a thing is related, when a name does not exist, if, from that which has a name, we derive a new name, and apply it to that with which the first is reciprocally connected, as in the aforesaid instances, when we derived the word 'winged' from 'wing' and from 'rudder'.

All relatives, then, if properly defined, have a correlative. I add this condition because, if that to which they are related is stated as haphazard and not accurately, the two are not found to be interdependent. Let me state what I mean more clearly. Even in the case of acknowledged correlatives, and where names exist for each, there will be no interdependence if one of the two is denoted, not by that name which expresses the correlative notion, but by one of irrelevant significance. The term 'slave', if defined as related, not to a master, but to a man, or a biped, or anything of that sort, is not reciprocally connected with that in relation to which it is defined, for the statement is not exact. Further, if one thing is said to be correlative with another, and the terminology used is correct, then, though all irrelevant attributes should be removed, and only that one attribute left in virtue of which it was correctly stated to be correlative with that other, the stated correlation will still exist. If the correlative of 'the slave' is said to be 'the master', then, though all irrelevant attributes of the said 'master', such as 'biped', 'receptive of knowledge', 'human', should be removed, and the attribute 'master' alone left, the stated correlation existing between him and the slave will remain the same, for it is of a master that a slave is said to be the slave. On the other hand, if, of two correlatives, one is not correctly termed, then, when all other attributes are removed and that alone is left in virtue of which it was stated to be correlative, the stated correlation will be found to have disappeared.

For suppose the correlative of 'the slave' should be said to be 'the man', or the correlative of 'the wing' is 'the bird'; if the attribute 'master' be withdrawn from 'the man', the correlation between 'the man' and 'the slave' will cease to exist, for if the man is not a master, the slave is not a slave. Similarly, if the attribute 'winged' be withdrawn from 'the bird', 'the wing' will no longer be relative; for if the so-called correlative is not winged, it follows that 'the wing' has no correlative.

Thus it is essential that the correlated terms should be exactly designated; if there is a name existing, the statement will be easy; if not, it is doubtless our duty to construct names. When the terminology is thus correct, it is evident that all correlatives are interdependent.

Correlatives are thought to come into existence simultaneously. This is for the most part true, as in the case of the double and the half. The existence of the half necessitates the existence of that of which it is a half. Similarly the existence of a master necessitates the existence of a slave, and that of a slave implies that of a master; these are merely instances of a general rule. Moreover, they cancel one another; for if there is no double it follows that there is no half, and vice versa; this rule also applies to all such correlatives. Yet it does not appear to be true in all cases that correlatives come into existence simultaneously. The object of knowledge would appear to exist before knowledge itself, for it is usually the case that we acquire knowledge of objects already existing; it would be difficult, if not impossible, to find a branch of knowledge the beginning of the existence of which was contemporaneous with that of its object.

Again, while the object of knowledge, if it ceases to exist, cancels at the same time the knowledge which was its correlative, the converse of this is not true. It is true that if the object of knowledge does not exist there can be no knowledge: for there will no longer be anything to know. Yet it is equally true that, if knowledge of a certain object does not exist, the object may nevertheless quite well exist. Thus, in the case of the squaring of the circle, if indeed that process is an object of knowledge, though it itself exists as an object of knowledge, yet the knowledge of it has not yet come into existence. Again, if all animals ceased to exist, there would be no knowledge, but there might yet be many objects of knowledge.

This is likewise the case with regard to perception: for the object of perception is, it appears, prior to the act of perception. If the perceptible is annihilated, perception also will cease to exist; but the annihilation of perception does not cancel the existence of the perceptible. For perception implies a body perceived and a body in which perception takes place. Now if that which is perceptible is annihilated, it follows that the body is annihilated, for the body is a perceptible thing; and if the body does not exist, it follows that perception also ceases to exist. Thus the annihilation of the perceptible involves that of perception.

But the annihilation of perception does not involve that of the perceptible. For if the animal is annihilated, it follows that perception also is annihilated, but perceptibles such as body, heat, sweetness, bitterness, and so on, will remain.

Again, perception is generated at the same time as the perceiving subject, for it comes into existence at the same time as the animal. But the perceptible surely exists before perception; for fire and water and such elements, out of which the animal is itself composed, exist before the animal is an animal at all, and before perception. Thus it would seem that the perceptible exists before perception.

It may be questioned whether it is true that no substance is relative, as seems to be the case, or whether exception is to be made in the case of certain secondary substances. With regard to primary substances, it is quite true that there is no such possibility, for neither wholes nor parts of primary substances are relative. The individual man or ox is not defined with reference to something external. Similarly with the parts: a particular hand or head is not defined as a particular hand or head of a particular person, but as the hand or head of a particular person. It is true also, for the most part at least, in the case of secondary substances; the species 'man' and the species 'ox' are not defined with reference to anything outside themselves. Wood, again, is only relative in so far as it is some one's property, not in so far as it is wood. It is plain, then, that in the cases mentioned substance is not relative. But with regard to some secondary substances there is a difference of opinion; thus, such terms as 'head' and 'hand' are defined with reference to that of which the things indicated are a part, and so it comes about that these appear to have a relative character. Indeed, if our definition of that which is relative was complete, it is very difficult, if not impossible, to prove that no substance is relative. If, however, our definition was not complete, if those things only are properly called relative in the case of which relation to an external object is a necessary condition of existence, perhaps some explanation of the dilemma may be found.

The former definition does indeed apply to all relatives, but the fact that a thing is explained with reference to something else does not make it essentially relative.

From this it is plain that, if a man definitely apprehends a relative thing, he will also definitely apprehend that to which it is relative. Indeed this is self-evident: for if a man knows that some particular thing is relative, assuming that we call that a relative in the case of which relation to something is a necessary condition of existence, he knows that also to which it is related. For if he does not know at all that to which it is related, he will not know whether or not it is relative. This is clear, moreover, in particular instances. If a man knows definitely that such and such a thing is 'double', he will also forthwith know definitely that of which it is the double. For if there is nothing definite of which he knows it to be the double, he does not know at all that it is double. Again, if he knows that a thing is more beautiful, it follows necessarily that he will forthwith definitely know that also than which it is more beautiful. He will not merely know indefinitely that it is more beautiful than something which is less beautiful, for this would be supposition, not knowledge. For if he does not know definitely that than which it is more beautiful, he can no longer claim to know definitely that it is more beautiful than something else which is less beautiful: for it might be that nothing was less beautiful. It is, therefore, evident that if a man apprehends some relative thing definitely, he necessarily knows that also definitely to which it is related.

Now the head, the hand, and such things are substances, and it is possible to know their essential character definitely, but it does not necessarily follow that we should know that to which they are related. It is not possible to know forthwith whose head or hand is meant. Thus these are not relatives, and, this being the case, it would be true to say that no substance is relative in character. It is perhaps a difficult matter, in such cases, to make a positive statement without more exhaustive examination, but to have raised questions with regard to details is not without advantage.

Part 8

By 'quality' I mean that in virtue of which people are said to be such and such.

Quality is a term that is used in many senses. One sort of quality let us call 'habit' or 'disposition'. Habit differs from disposition in being more lasting and more firmly established. The various kinds of knowledge and of virtue are habits, for knowledge, even when acquired only in a moderate degree, is, it is agreed, abiding in its character and difficult to displace, unless some great mental upheaval takes place, through disease or any such cause. The virtues, also, such as justice, self-restraint, and so on, are not easily dislodged or dismissed, so as to give place to vice.

By a disposition, on the other hand, we mean a condition that is easily changed and quickly gives place to its opposite. Thus, heat, cold, disease, health, and so on are dispositions. For a man is disposed in one way or another with reference to these, but quickly changes, becoming cold instead of warm, ill instead of well. So it is with all other dispositions also, unless through lapse of time a disposition has itself become inveterate and almost impossible to dislodge: in which case we should perhaps go so far as to call it a habit.

It is evident that men incline to call those conditions habits which are of a more or less permanent type and difficult to displace; for those who are not retentive of knowledge, but volatile, are not said to have such and such a 'habit' as regards knowledge, yet they are disposed, we may say, either better or worse, towards knowledge. Thus habit differs from disposition in this, that while the latter in ephemeral, the former is permanent and difficult to alter.

Habits are at the same time dispositions, but dispositions are not necessarily habits. For those who have some specific habit may be said also, in virtue of that habit, to be thus or thus disposed; but those who are disposed in some specific way have not in all cases the corresponding habit.

Another sort of quality is that in virtue of which, for example, we call men good boxers or runners, or healthy or sickly: in fact it includes all those terms which refer to inborn capacity or incapacity. Such things are not predicated of a person in virtue of his disposition, but in virtue of his inborn capacity or incapacity to do something with ease or to avoid defeat of any kind. Persons are called good boxers or good runners, not in virtue of such and such a disposition, but in virtue of an inborn capacity to accomplish something with ease. Men are called healthy in virtue of the inborn capacity of easy resistance to those unhealthy influences that may ordinarily arise; unhealthy, in virtue of the lack of this capacity. Similarly with regard to softness and hardness. Hardness is predicated of a thing because it has that capacity

41

of resistance which enables it to withstand disintegration; softness, again, is predicated of a thing by reason of the lack of that capacity.

A third class within this category is that of affective qualities and affections. Sweetness, bitterness, sourness, are examples of this sort of quality, together with all that is akin to these; heat, moreover, and cold, whiteness, and blackness are affective qualities. It is evident that these are qualities, for those things that possess them are themselves said to be such and such by reason of their presence. Honey is called sweet because it contains sweetness; the body is called white because it contains whiteness; and so in all other cases.

The term 'affective quality' is not used as indicating that those things which admit these qualities are affected in any way. Honey is not called sweet because it is affected in a specific way, nor is this what is meant in any other instance. Similarly heat and cold are called affective qualities, not because those things which admit them are affected. What is meant is that these said qualities are capable of producing an 'affection' in the way of perception. For sweetness has the power of affecting the sense of taste; heat, that of touch; and so it is with the rest of these qualities.

Whiteness and blackness, however, and the other colours, are not said to be affective qualities in this sense, but because they themselves are the results of an affection. It is plain that many changes of colour take place because of affections. When a man is ashamed, he blushes; when he is afraid, he becomes pale, and so on. So true is this, that when a man is by nature liable to such affections, arising from some concomitance of elements in his constitution, it is a probable inference that he has the corresponding complexion of skin. For the same disposition of bodily elements, which in the former instance was momentarily present in the case of an access of shame, might be a result of a man's natural temperament, so as to produce the corresponding colouring also as a natural characteristic. All conditions, therefore, of this kind, if caused by certain permanent and lasting affections, are called affective qualities. For pallor and duskiness of complexion are called qualities, inasmuch as we are said to be such and such in virtue of them, not only if they originate in natural constitution, but also if they come about through long disease or sunburn, and are difficult to remove, or indeed remain throughout life. For in the same way we are said to be such and such because of these.

Those conditions, however, which arise from causes which may easily be rendered ineffective or speedily removed, are called, not qualities, but affections: for we are not said to be such in virtue of them. The man who blushes through shame is not said to be a constitutional blusher, nor is the man who becomes pale through fear said to be constitutionally pale. He is said rather to have been affected.

Thus such conditions are called affections, not qualities. In like manner there are affective qualities and affections of the soul. That temper with which a man is born and which has its origin in certain deep-seated affections is called a quality. I mean such conditions as insanity, irascibility, and so on: for people are said to be mad or irascible in virtue of these. Similarly those abnormal psychic states which are not inborn, but arise from the concomitance of certain other elements, and are difficult to remove, or altogether permanent, are called qualities, for in virtue of them men are said to be such and such.

Those, however, which arise from causes easily rendered ineffective are called affections, not qualities. Suppose that a man is irritable when vexed: he is not even spoken of as a bad-tempered man, when in such circumstances he loses his temper somewhat, but rather is said to be affected. Such conditions are therefore termed, not qualities, but affections.

The fourth sort of quality is figure and the shape that belongs to a thing; and besides this, straightness and curvedness and any other qualities of this type; each of these defines a thing as being such and such. Because it is triangular or quadrangular a thing is said to have a specific character, or again because it is straight or curved; in fact a thing's shape in every case gives rise to a qualification of it.

Rarity and density, roughness and smoothness, seem to be terms indicating quality: yet these, it would appear, really belong to a class different from that of quality. For it is rather a certain relative position of the parts composing the thing thus qualified which, it appears, is indicated by each of these terms. A thing is dense, owing to the fact that its parts are closely combined with one another; rare, because there are interstices between the parts; smooth, because its parts lie, so to speak, evenly; rough, because some parts project beyond others.

There may be other sorts of quality, but those that are most properly so called have, we may safely say, been enumerated.

These, then, are qualities, and the things that take their name from them as derivatives, or are in some other way dependent on them, are said to be qualified in some specific way. In most, indeed in almost all cases, the name of that which is qualified is derived from that of the quality. Thus the terms 'whiteness', 'grammar', 'justice', give us the adjectives 'white', 'grammatical', 'just', and so on.

There are some cases, however, in which, as the quality under consideration has no name, it is impossible that those possessed of it should have a name that is derivative. For instance, the name given to the runner or boxer, who is so called in virtue of an inborn capacity, is not derived from that of any quality; for both those capacities have no name assigned to them. In this, the inborn capacity is distinct from the science, with reference to which men are called, e.g. boxers or wrestlers. Such a science is classed as a disposition; it has a name, and is called 'boxing' or 'wrestling' as the case may be, and the name given to those disposed in this way is derived from that of the science. Sometimes, even though a name exists for the quality, that which takes its character from the quality has a name that is not a derivative. For instance, the upright man takes his character from the possession of the quality of integrity, but the name given him is not derived from the word 'integrity'. Yet this does not occur often.

We may therefore state that those things are said to be possessed of some specific quality which have a name derived from that of the aforesaid quality, or which are in some other way dependent on it.

One quality may be the contrary of another; thus justice is the contrary of injustice, whiteness of blackness, and so on. The things, also, which are said to be such and such in virtue of these qualities, may be contrary the one to the other; for that which is unjust is contrary to that which is just, that which is white to that which is black. This, however, is not always the case. Red, yellow, and such colours, though qualities, have no contraries.

If one of two contraries is a quality, the other will also be a quality. This will be evident from particular instances, if we apply the names used to denote the other categories; for instance, granted that justice is the contrary of injustice and justice is a quality, injustice will also be a quality: neither quantity, nor relation, nor place, nor indeed any other category but that of quality, will be applicable properly to injustice. So it is with all other contraries falling under the category of quality.

Qualities admit of variation of degree. Whiteness is predicated of one thing in a greater or less degree than of another. This is also the case with reference to justice. Moreover, one and the same thing may exhibit a quality in a greater degree than it did before: if a thing is white, it may become whiter.

Though this is generally the case, there are exceptions. For if we should say that justice admitted of variation of degree, difficulties might ensue, and this is true with regard to all those qualities which are dispositions. There are some, indeed, who dispute the possibility of variation here. They maintain that justice and health cannot very well admit of variation of degree themselves, but that people vary in the degree in which they possess these qualities, and that this is the case with grammatical learning and all those qualities which are classed as dispositions. However that may be, it is an incontrovertible fact that the things which in virtue of these qualities are said to be what they are vary in the degree in which they possess them; for one man is said to be better versed in grammar, or more healthy or just, than another, and so on.

The qualities expressed by the terms 'triangular' and 'quadrangular' do not appear to admit of variation of degree, nor indeed do any that have to do with figure. For those things to which the definition of the triangle or circle is applicable are all equally triangular or circular. Those, on the other hand, to which the same definition is not applicable, cannot be said to differ from one another in degree; the square is no more a circle than the rectangle, for to neither is the definition of the circle appropriate. In short, if the definition of the term proposed is not applicable to both objects, they cannot be compared. Thus it is not all qualities which admit of variation of degree.

Whereas none of the characteristics I have mentioned are peculiar to quality, the fact that likeness and unlikeness can be predicated with reference to quality only, gives to that category its distinctive feature. One thing is like another only with reference to that in virtue of which it is such and such; thus this forms the peculiar mark of quality.

We must not be disturbed because it may be argued that, though proposing to discuss the category of quality, we have included in it many relative terms. We did say that habits and dispositions were relative. In practically all such cases the genus is relative, the individual not. Thus knowledge, as a genus, is explained by reference to something else, for we mean a knowledge of something. But particular branches of knowledge are not thus explained. The knowledge of grammar is not relative to anything external, nor is the knowledge of music, but these, if relative at all, are relative only in virtue of their genera; thus grammar is said be the knowledge of something, not the grammar of something; similarly music is the knowledge of something, not the music of something.

Thus individual branches of knowledge are not relative. And it is because we possess these individual branches of knowledge that we are said to be such and such. It is these that we actually possess: we are called experts because we possess knowledge in some particular branch. Those particular branches, therefore, of knowledge, in virtue of which we are sometimes said to be such and such, are themselves qualities, and are not relative. Further, if anything should happen to fall within both the category of quality and that of relation, there would be nothing extraordinary in classing it under both these heads.

Section 3

Part 9

Action and affection both admit of contraries and also of variation of degree. Heating is the contrary of cooling, being heated of being cooled, being glad of being vexed. Thus they admit of contraries. They also admit of variation of degree: for it is possible to heat in a greater or less degree; also to be heated in a greater or less degree. Thus action and affection also admit of variation of degree. So much, then, is stated with regard to these categories.

We spoke, moreover, of the category of position when we were dealing with that of relation, and stated that such terms derived their names from those of the corresponding attitudes.

As for the rest, time, place, state, since they are easily intelligible, I say no more about them than was said at the beginning, that in the category of state are included such states as 'shod', 'armed', in that of place 'in the Lyceum' and so on, as was explained before.

Part 10

The proposed categories have, then, been adequately dealt with. We must next explain the various senses in which the term 'opposite' is used. Things are said to be opposed in four senses: (i) as correlatives to one another, (ii) as contraries to one another, (iii) as privatives to positives, (iv) as affirmatives to negatives.

Let me sketch my meaning in outline. An instance of the use of the word 'opposite' with reference to correlatives is afforded by the expressions 'double' and 'half'; with reference to contraries by 'bad' and 'good'. Opposites in the sense of 'privatives' and 'positives' are 'blindness' and 'sight'; in the sense of affirmatives and negatives, the propositions 'he sits', 'he does not sit'.

(i) Pairs of opposites which fall under the category of relation are explained by a reference of the one to the other, the reference being indicated by the preposition 'of' or by some other preposition. Thus, double is a relative term, for that which is double is explained as the double of something. Knowledge, again, is the opposite of the thing known, in the same sense; and the thing known also is explained by its relation to its opposite, knowledge. For the thing known is explained as that which is known by something, that is, by knowledge. Such things, then, as are opposite the one to the other in the sense of being correlatives are explained by a reference of the one to the other.

(ii) Pairs of opposites which are contraries are not in any way interdependent, but are contrary the one to the other. The good is not spoken of as the good of the bad, but as the contrary of the bad, nor is white spoken of as the white of the black, but as the contrary of the black. These two types of opposition are therefore distinct. Those contraries which are such that the subjects in which they are naturally present, or of which they are predicated, must necessarily contain either the one or the other of them, have no intermediate, but those in the case of which no such necessity obtains, always have an intermediate. Thus disease and health are naturally present in the body of an animal, and it is necessary that either the one or the other should be present in the body of an animal. Odd and even, again, are predicated of number, and it is necessary that the one or the other should be present in numbers. Now there is no intermediate between the terms of either of these two pairs. On the other hand, in those contraries with regard to which no such necessity obtains, we find an intermediate. Blackness and whiteness are naturally present in the body, but it is not necessary that either the one or the other should be present in the body, inasmuch as it is not true to say that everybody must be white or black. Badness and goodness, again, are predicated of man, and of many other things, but it is not necessary that either the one quality or the other should be present in that of which they are predicated: it is not true to say that everything that may be good or bad must be either good or bad. These pairs of contraries have intermediates: the intermediates between white and black are grey, sallow, and all the other colours that come between; the intermediate between good and bad is that which is neither the one nor the other.

Some intermediate qualities have names, such as grey and sallow and all the other colours that come between white and black; in other cases, however, it is not easy to name the intermediate, but we must define it as that which is not either extreme, as in the case of that which is neither good nor bad, neither just nor unjust.

(iii) 'privatives' and 'positives' have reference to the same subject. Thus, sight and blindness have reference to the eye. It is a universal rule that each of a pair of opposites of this type has reference to that to which the particular 'positive' is natural. We say that that is capable of some particular faculty or possession has suffered privation when the faculty or possession in question is in no way present in that in which, and at the time at which, it should naturally be present. We do not call that toothless which has not teeth, or that blind which has not sight, but rather that which has not teeth or sight at the time when by nature it should. For there are some creatures which from birth are without sight, or without teeth, but these are not called toothless or blind.

51

To be without some faculty or to possess it is not the same as the corresponding 'privative' or 'positive'. 'Sight' is a 'positive', 'blindness' a 'privative', but 'to possess sight' is not equivalent to 'sight', 'to be blind' is not equivalent to 'blindness'. Blindness is a 'privative', to be blind is to be in a state of privation, but is not a 'privative'. Moreover, if 'blindness' were equivalent to 'being blind', both would be predicated of the same subject; but though a man is said to be blind, he is by no means said to be blindness.

To be in a state of 'possession' is, it appears, the opposite of being in a state of 'privation', just as 'positives' and 'privatives' themselves are opposite. There is the same type of antithesis in both cases; for just as blindness is opposed to sight, so is being blind opposed to having sight.

That which is affirmed or denied is not itself affirmation or denial. By 'affirmation' we mean an affirmative proposition, by 'denial' a negative. Now, those facts which form the matter of the affirmation or denial are not propositions; yet these two are said to be opposed in the same sense as the affirmation and denial, for in this case also the type of antithesis is the same. For as the affirmation is opposed to the denial, as in the two propositions 'he sits', 'he does not sit', so also the fact which constitutes the matter of the proposition in one case is opposed to that in the other, his sitting, that is to say, to his not sitting.

It is evident that 'positives' and 'privatives' are not opposed each to each in the same sense as relatives. The one is not explained by reference to the other; sight is not sight of blindness, nor is any other preposition used to indicate the relation. Similarly blindness is not said to be blindness of sight, but rather, privation of sight. Relatives, moreover, reciprocate; if blindness, therefore, were a relative, there would be a reciprocity of relation between it and that with which it was correlative. But this is not the case. Sight is not called the sight of blindness.

That those terms which fall under the heads of 'positives' and 'privatives' are not opposed each to each as contraries, either, is plain from the following facts: Of a pair of contraries such that they have no intermediate, one or the other must needs be present in the subject in which they naturally subsist, or of which they are predicated; for it is those, as we proved, in the case of which this necessity obtains, that have no intermediate. Moreover, we cited health and disease, odd and even, as instances. But those contraries which have an intermediate are not subject to any such necessity. It is not necessary that every substance, receptive of such qualities, should be either black or white, cold or hot, for something intermediate between these contraries may very well be present in the subject. We proved, moreover, that those contraries have an intermediate in the case of which the said necessity does not obtain. Yet when one of the two contraries is a constitutive property of the subject, as it is a constitutive property of fire to be hot, of snow to be white, it is necessary determinately that one of the two contraries, not one or the other, should be present in the subject; for fire cannot be cold, or snow black. Thus, it is not the case here that one of the two must needs be present in every subject receptive of these qualities, but only in that subject of which the one forms a constitutive property. Moreover, in such cases it is one member of the pair determinately, and not either the one or the other, which must be present.

In the case of 'positives' and 'privatives', on the other hand, neither of the aforesaid statements holds good. For it is not necessary that a subject receptive of the qualities should always have either the one or the other; that which has not yet advanced to the state when sight is natural is not said either to be blind or to see. Thus 'positives' and 'privatives' do not belong to that class of contraries which consists of those which have no intermediate. On the other hand, they do not belong either to that class which consists of contraries which have an intermediate. For under certain conditions it is necessary that either the one or the other should form part of the constitution of every appropriate subject. For when a thing has reached the stage when it is by nature capable of sight, it will be said either to see or to be blind, and that in an indeterminate sense, signifying that the capacity may be either present or absent; for it is not necessary either that it should see or that it should be blind, but that it should be either in the one state or in the other. Yet in the case of those contraries which have an intermediate we found that it was never necessary that either the one or the other should be present in every appropriate subject, but only that in certain subjects one of the pair should be present, and that in a determinate sense. It is, therefore, plain that 'positives' and 'privatives' are not opposed each to each in either of the senses in which contraries are opposed.

Again, in the case of contraries, it is possible that there should be changes from either into the other, while the subject retains its identity, unless indeed one of the contraries is a constitutive property of that subject, as heat is of fire. For it is possible that that that which is healthy should become diseased, that which is white, black, that which is cold, hot, that which is good, bad, that which is bad, good. The bad man, if he is being brought into a better way of life and thought, may make some advance, however slight, and if he should once improve, even ever so little, it is plain that he might change completely, or at any rate make very great progress; for a man becomes more and more easily moved to virtue, however small the improvement was at first. It is, therefore, natural to suppose that he will make yet greater progress than he has made in the past; and as this process goes on, it will change him completely and establish him in the contrary state, provided he is not hindered by lack of time. In the case of 'positives' and 'privatives', however, change in both directions is impossible. There may be a change from possession to privation, but not from privation to possession. The man who has become blind does not regain his sight; the man who has become bald does not regain his hair; the man who has lost his teeth does not grow a new set.

(iv) Statements opposed as affirmation and negation belong manifestly to a class which is distinct, for in this case, and in this case only, it is necessary for the one opposite to be true and the other false.

Neither in the case of contraries, nor in the case of correlatives, nor in the case of 'positives' and 'privatives', is it necessary for one to be true and the other false. Health and disease are contraries: neither of them is true or false. 'Double' and 'half' are opposed to each other as correlatives: neither of them is true or false. The case is the same, of course, with regard to 'positives' and 'privatives' such as 'sight' and 'blindness'. In short, where there is no sort of combination of words, truth and falsity have no place, and all the opposites we have mentioned so far consist of simple words.

At the same time, when the words which enter into opposed statements are contraries, these, more than any other set of opposites, would seem to claim this characteristic. 'Socrates is ill' is the contrary of 'Socrates is well', but not even of such composite expressions is it true to say that one of the pair must always be true and the other false. For if Socrates exists, one will be true and the other false, but if he does not exist, both will be false; for neither 'Socrates is ill' nor 'Socrates is well' is true, if Socrates does not exist at all.

In the case of 'positives' and 'privatives', if the subject does not exist at all, neither proposition is true, but even if the subject exists, it is not always the fact that one is true and the other false. For 'Socrates has sight' is the opposite of 'Socrates is blind' in the sense of the word 'opposite' which applies to possession and privation. Now if Socrates exists, it is not necessary that one should be true and the other false, for when he is not yet able to acquire the power of vision, both are false, as also if Socrates is altogether non-existent.

But in the case of affirmation and negation, whether the subject exists or not, one is always false and the other true. For manifestly, if Socrates exists, one of the two propositions 'Socrates is ill', 'Socrates is not ill', is true, and the other false. This is likewise the case if he does not exist; for if he does not exist, to say that he is ill is false, to say that he is not ill is true. Thus it is in the case of those opposites only, which are opposite in the sense in which the term is used with reference to affirmation and negation, that the rule holds good, that one of the pair must be true and the other false.

Part 11

That the contrary of a good is an evil is shown by induction: the contrary of health is disease, of courage, cowardice, and so on. But the contrary of an evil is sometimes a good, sometimes an evil. For defect, which is an evil, has excess for its contrary, this also being an evil, and the mean, which is a good, is equally the contrary of the one and of the other. It is only in a few cases, however, that we see instances of this: in most, the contrary of an evil is a good.

In the case of contraries, it is not always necessary that if one exists the other should also exist: for if all become healthy there will be health and no disease, and again, if everything turns white, there will be white, but no black. Again, since the fact that Socrates is ill is the contrary of the fact that Socrates is well, and two contrary conditions cannot both obtain in one and the same individual at the same time, both these contraries could not exist at once: for if that Socrates was well was a fact, then that Socrates was ill could not possibly be one.

It is plain that contrary attributes must needs be present in subjects which belong to the same species or genus. Disease and health require as their subject the body of an animal; white and black require a body, without further qualification; justice and injustice require as their subject the human soul.

Moreover, it is necessary that pairs of contraries should in all cases either belong to the same genus or belong to contrary genera or be themselves genera. White and black belong to the same genus, colour; justice and injustice, to contrary genera, virtue and vice; while good and evil do not belong to genera, but are themselves actual genera, with terms under them.

Part 12

There are four senses in which one thing can be said to be 'prior' to another. Primarily and most properly the term has reference to time: in this sense the word is used to indicate that one thing is older or more ancient than another, for the expressions 'older' and 'more ancient' imply greater length of time.

Secondly, one thing is said to be 'prior' to another when the sequence of their being cannot be reversed. In this sense 'one' is 'prior' to 'two'. For if 'two' exists, it follows directly that 'one' must exist, but if 'one' exists, it does not follow necessarily that 'two' exists: thus the sequence subsisting cannot be reversed. It is agreed, then, that when the sequence of two things cannot be reversed, then that one on which the other depends is called 'prior' to that other.

In the third place, the term 'prior' is used with reference to any order, as in the case of science and of oratory. For in sciences which use demonstration there is that which is prior and that which is posterior in order; in geometry, the elements are prior to the propositions; in reading and writing, the letters of the alphabet are prior to the syllables. Similarly, in the case of speeches, the exordium is prior in order to the narrative.

Besides these senses of the word, there is a fourth. That which is better and more honourable is said to have a natural priority. In common parlance men speak of those whom they honour and love as 'coming first' with them. This sense of the word is perhaps the most far-fetched.

Such, then, are the different senses in which the term 'prior' is used.

Yet it would seem that besides those mentioned there is yet another. For in those things, the being of each of which implies that of the other, that which is in any way the cause may reasonably be said to be by nature 'prior' to the effect. It is plain that there are instances of this. The fact of the being of a man carries with it the truth of the proposition that he is, and the implication is reciprocal: for if a man is, the proposition wherein we allege that he is true, and conversely, if the proposition wherein we allege that he is true, then he is. The true proposition, however, is in no way the cause of the being of the man, but the fact of the man's being does seem somehow to be the cause of the truth of the proposition, for the truth or falsity of the proposition depends on the fact of the man's being or not being.

Thus the word 'prior' may be used in five senses.

Part 13

The term 'simultaneous' is primarily and most appropriately applied to those things the genesis of the one of which is simultaneous with that of the other; for in such cases neither is prior or posterior to the other. Such things are said to be simultaneous in point of time. Those things, again, are 'simultaneous' in point of nature, the being of each of which involves that of the other, while at the same time neither is the cause of the other's being. This is the case with regard to the double and the half, for these are reciprocally dependent, since, if there is a double, there is also a half, and if there is a half, there is also a double, while at the same time neither is the cause of the being of the other.

Again, those species which are distinguished one from another and opposed one to another within the same genus are said to be 'simultaneous' in nature. I mean those species which are distinguished each from each by one and the same method of division. Thus the 'winged' species is simultaneous with the 'terrestrial' and the 'water' species. These are distinguished within the same genus, and are opposed each to each, for the genus 'animal' has the 'winged', the 'terrestrial', and the 'water' species, and no one of these is prior or posterior to another; on the contrary, all such things appear to be 'simultaneous' in nature. Each of these also, the terrestrial, the winged, and the water species, can be divided again into subspecies. Those species, then, also will be 'simultaneous' in point of nature, which, belonging to the same genus, are distinguished each from each by one and the same method of differentiation.

But genera are prior to species, for the sequence of their being cannot be reversed. If there is the species 'water-animal', there will be the genus 'animal', but granted the being of the genus 'animal', it does not follow necessarily that there will be the species 'water-animal'.

Those things, therefore, are said to be 'simultaneous' in nature, the being of each of which involves that of the other, while at the same time neither is in any way the cause of the other's being; those species, also, which are distinguished each from each and opposed within the same genus. Those things, moreover, are 'simultaneous' in the unqualified sense of the word which come into being at the same time.

Part 14

There are six sorts of movement: generation, destruction, increase, diminution, alteration, and change of place.

It is evident in all but one case that all these sorts of movement are distinct each from each. Generation is distinct from destruction, increase and change of place from diminution, and so on. But in the case of alteration it may be argued that the process necessarily implies one or other of the other five sorts of motion. This is not true, for we may say that all affections, or nearly all, produce in us an alteration which is distinct from all other sorts of motion, for that which is affected need not suffer either increase or diminution or any of the other sorts of motion. Thus alteration is a distinct sort of motion; for, if it were not, the thing altered would not only be altered, but would forthwith necessarily suffer increase or diminution or some one of the other sorts of motion in addition; which as a matter of fact is not the case. Similarly that which was undergoing the process of increase or was subject to some other sort of motion would, if alteration were not a distinct form of motion, necessarily be subject to alteration also. But there are some things which undergo increase but yet not alteration. The square, for instance, if a gnomon is applied to it, undergoes increase but not alteration, and so it is with all other figures of this sort. Alteration and increase, therefore, are distinct.

Speaking generally, rest is the contrary of motion. But the different forms of motion have their own contraries in other forms; thus destruction is the contrary of generation, diminution of increase, rest in a place, of change of place. As for this last, change in the reverse direction would seem to be most truly its contrary; thus motion upwards is the contrary of motion downwards and vice versa.

In the case of that sort of motion which yet remains, of those that have been enumerated, it is not easy to state what is its contrary. It appears to have no contrary, unless one should define the contrary here also either as 'rest in its quality' or as 'change in the direction of the contrary quality', just as we defined the contrary of change of place either as rest in a place or as change in the reverse direction. For a thing is altered when change of quality takes place; therefore either rest in its quality or change in the direction of the contrary may be called the contrary of this qualitative form of motion. In this way becoming white is the contrary of becoming black; there is alteration in the contrary direction, since a change of a qualitative nature takes place.

Part 15

The term 'to have' is used in various senses. In the first place it is used with reference to habit or disposition or any other quality, for we are said to 'have' a piece of knowledge or a virtue. Then, again, it has reference to quantity, as, for instance, in the case of a man's height; for he is said to 'have' a height of three or four cubits. It is used, moreover, with regard to apparel, a man being said to 'have' a coat or tunic; or in respect of something which we have on a part of ourselves, as a ring on the hand: or in respect of something which is a part of us, as hand or foot. The term refers also to content, as in the case of a vessel and wheat, or of a jar and wine; a jar is said to 'have' wine, and a corn-measure wheat. The expression in such cases has reference to content. Or it refers to that which has been acquired; we are said to 'have' a house or a field. A man is also said to 'have' a wife, and a wife a husband, and this appears to be the most remote meaning of the term, for by the use of it we mean simply that the husband lives with the wife.

Other senses of the word might perhaps be found, but the most ordinary ones have all been enumerated.

SIMPLE APPREHENSION - COMMENTARY

Intentionality - referential to another. Knowledge is *of something*.
> **First Intention** - an actual being in the world, e.g., a dog.
> **Second Intention** - a mental being, e.g., the idea of a dog.

Sign - represents another.
Signatum - the thing represented.

	Material Sign - has its own existence other than being a sign.	**Formal Sign** - is only a sign and nothing else. Only ideas.
Natural Sign - not man-made.	Smoke indicating fire.	Ideas.
Artificial Sign - man-made.	A "STOP" sign, or the word "stop."	X

Concept - an intellectual abstraction of the essence of a thing.
> **Comprehension** - the definition of the concept, e.g., "rational animal."
> **Extension** - the things to which the concept applies, e.g., "all humans."

> **Simple Concept**: "apple"
> **Complex Concept**: "green apple"

> **Concrete Concept**: "human"
> **Abstract Concept**: "humanity"

> **Collective Concept**: "All the feathers weigh 50 pounds."
> **Divisive Concept**: "Each of the feathers can be used to tickle someone."

[handwritten note in left margin: COME IN SETS]

Material Object - the actual being which is considered by the mind, e.g., "a door."
Formal Object - the aspect or part which is being considered, e.g., "the color of the door."

Term - a verbal or written expression of a concept. Conventional, i.e., agreed upon, as opposed to concepts, which are natural.

> **Subject** - the term being spoken about.
> **Predicate** - what is being said about the subject.
> **Copula** - the verb "is," which joins Subject and Predicate.

<u>Subject</u>   <u>Copula</u>   <u>Predicate</u>
The king   is   a nice guy.

Univocal Terms - used in exactly the same sense:
   "The Poodle *barks* and the Doberman *barks*."
Equivocal Terms - used in totally different senses:
   "The Doberman *barks* at the *bark* of the tree."
Analogical Terms - used in similar, not identical senses:
   "You seem *healthy*. Are eggs *healthy* for you?"

THE CATEGORIES - HOW SUBJECTS CAN BE

Substance - the nature or essence of the thing. <u>"Man."</u>
   Primary Substance - the actual existing thing. <u>"Socrates."</u>
   Secondary Substance - a primary substance's nature. <u>"Man."</u>
Quantity - how much or how many. <u>"Six feet tall."</u>
Quality - how it is - a qualification. <u>"Tan."</u>
Relation - how it is connected to another. <u>"Teacher of Plato."</u>
Action - what it is doing. <u>"Teaching."</u>
Passion - what is being done to it. <u>"Being hated."</u>
Location - where it is. <u>"In Athens."</u>
Position - how it is arranged. <u>"Standing up."</u>
Time - when it is. <u>"A long time ago."</u>
Possession - how it is clothed or adorned. <u>"Wearing a toga."</u>

(handwritten left margin brace labeled: Accidents)

THE PREDICABLES - HOW PREDICATES CAN BE

Genus - a broader classification. <u>"Animal."</u>
Specific Difference – what differentiates a species. <u>"Rational."</u>
Species - a stricter classification. <u>"Rational animal."</u>
Property - a non-definitive characteristic of a species. <u>"Risible."</u>
Accident - a characteristic shared by other species. <u>"Living."</u>

FORMING DEFINITIONS

Contradictory Opposition - leaves nothing out, has no overlap; <u>red and not-red</u>
Contrary Opposition - leaves things out; <u>red and white</u>

<u>**Nominal Definitions**</u> - define the **word**; 3 types:

Conventional Definition - what we have agreed upon as the meaning of the word; found in dictionaries; uses synonyms:
<u>Human</u>: any individual of the genus Homo, esp. a member of the species Homo sapiens. (dictionary.com)

Etymological Definition - looks at the source of the term linguistically, based on its roots in the same or other languages:
<u>Human</u>: c.1250, from M.Fr. humain "of or belonging to man," from L. humanus, probably related to homo (gen. hominis) "man," and to humus "earth," on notion of "earthly beings," as opposed to the gods (cf. Heb. adam "man," from adamah "ground"). (etymonline.com)

Stipulative Definition - agreed upon for the sake of argument:
<u>Human</u>: let's say for the sake of argument that a human is defined as a laughing animal.

<u>**Real Definitions**</u> - define the **thing** in its nature.

Essential Definition - genus + specific difference:
<u>Human</u> - rational animal

Descriptive Definition - (genus) + properties or accidents:
<u>Human</u> - a thing with two legs, 10 fingers, hair...

Extrinsic Cause - defines according to the thing's purpose:
<u>Hammer</u> - a thing made to hit stuff with

Material Cause - defines according to what a thing is made of:
<u>Human</u> - a bunch of water, carbon, fat, bones, etc.

Simple Apprehension – Supplement
Sometimes, Area Woman Just Feels...

theonion.com - MARCH 20, 2010 | ISSUE 46•11

BELMONT, NH—Stating that she wasn't in the best place right now, and that things have been sort of you know, Belmont resident Megan Slota announced Thursday that sometimes she just feels....

Due to a general sense of…well, it's hard to explain, the 28-year-old dental hygienist reported that she just needed to work some stuff out, and that she would probably be a little I don't know for a couple weeks or so.

"It's not anybody's fault, honestly," said Slota, standing in her kitchen and holding a mug of tea with both hands. "Sometimes I just get like this where it's like I'm not, I guess, whatever. We don't have to get into it right now."

Added Slota, "I'm really, like, argh, I don't know."

After that thing with Dave on Thursday, people were concerned that Slota was in a weird place, which she initially denied. But Slota later admitted that she was just taking some time to figure things out and needed a little space, but it's not like she wanted people to leave her alone or anything like that.

"I had a really good talk with Debra," Slota said. "She's such a good friend. It's good to know I have someone like her. It's just a crazy time right now. And I've been really busy with work, too, so that hasn't helped."

While admitting that it must suck to have to deal with her lately, Slota said that she appreciates everyone's patience while she sorts all of this stuff out. Sources close to the sort of spacey, sort of—oh gosh, what would you even call it— distracted woman confirm that it's always the same this time of year, because of her dad.

"I worry about Megan," longtime friend Alex Polson said. "Times like this, she can get a little strange. Not strange strange, but still kind of strange where you're like, 'Huh?' But you know what? She's tough. She'll get through all this and be back to her old self in no time."

Though she's been kind of blah lately, especially at the family thing where she had to be on her best behavior, friends and coworkers have been understanding about what's going on with her, and want to let her know they're there if she needs help moving, or needs someone to go shopping with her, or just wants to hang out and not talk about the thing that happened with Samantha last week.

"You know, it's like when you're just," Slota said. "You feel one way but then you're also sort of, I don't know, maybe it's just one of those things. And you don't want to force it, right? I feel like you just have to accept it sometimes, I guess."

"It is what it is," she added.

Regardless of the thing that's, oh, whatever, it'll pass eventually, Slota maintained that she's forging ahead and taking things one day at a time.

Dr. Andrei Robinson, author of the book It's, Well, I'm Not Sure How To Describe It, Really, says that Slota's condition is not uncommon. "As a therapist, I'm seeing more and more patients with problems and conditions related to Ms. Slota's," Dr. Robinson said. "But ultimately, there's not a lot I can do for them. It's just another facet of this, whatever it is. You can't understand the, you know, well, anything, really. It's all too much sometimes, but it's her deal. She's got to work through it. We've all been there, right?"

"I don't know," Dr. Robinson added. "Does that make sense?"

From Lewis Carrol's *Alice's Adventures in Wonderland*

As there seemed to be no chance of getting her hands up to her head, she tried to get her head down to them, and was delighted to find that her neck would bend about easily in any direction, like a serpent. She had just succeeded in curving it down into a graceful zigzag, and was going to dive in among the leaves, which she found to be nothing but the tops of the trees under which she had been wandering, when a sharp hiss made her draw back in a hurry: a large pigeon had flown into her face, and was beating her violently with its wings.

`Serpent!' screamed the Pigeon.

`I'm NOT a serpent!' said Alice indignantly. `Let me alone!'

`Serpent, I say again!' repeated the Pigeon, but in a more subdued tone, and added with a kind of sob, `I've tried every way, and nothing seems to suit them!'

`I haven't the least idea what you're talking about,' said Alice.

`I've tried the roots of trees, and I've tried banks, and I've tried hedges,' the Pigeon went on, without attending to her; `but those serpents! There's no pleasing them!'

Alice was more and more puzzled, but she thought there was no use in saying anything more till the Pigeon had finished.

`As if it wasn't trouble enough hatching the eggs,' said the Pigeon; `but I must be on the look-out for serpents night and day! Why, I haven't had a wink of sleep these three weeks!'

`I'm very sorry you've been annoyed,' said Alice, who was beginning to see its meaning.

`And just as I'd taken the highest tree in the wood,' continued the Pigeon, raising its voice to a shriek, `and just as I was thinking I should be free of them at last, they must needs come wriggling down from the sky! Ugh, Serpent!'

`But I'm NOT a serpent, I tell you!' said Alice. `I'm a--I'm a--'

`Well! WHAT are you?' said the Pigeon. `I can see you're trying to invent something!'

`I--I'm a little girl,' said Alice, rather doubtfully, as she remembered the number of changes she had gone through that day.

`A likely story indeed!' said the Pigeon in a tone of the deepest contempt. `I've seen a good many little girls in my time, but never ONE with such a neck as that! No, no! You're a serpent; and there's no use denying it. I suppose you'll be telling me next that you never tasted an egg!'

`I HAVE tasted eggs, certainly,' said Alice, who was a very truthful child; `but little girls eat eggs quite as much as serpents do, you know.'

`I don't believe it,' said the Pigeon; `but if they do, why then they're a kind of serpent, that's all I can say.'

This was such a new idea to Alice, that she was quite silent for a minute or two, which gave the Pigeon the opportunity of adding, `You're looking for eggs, I know THAT well enough; and what does it matter to me whether you're a little girl or a serpent?'

* * *

Then the Queen left off, quite out of breath, and said to Alice, "Have you seen the Mock Turtle yet?"
"No," said Alice. "I don't even know what a Mock Turtle is."
"It's the thing Mock Turtle Soup is made from," said the Queen.

LOGICAL FALLACIES - TEXT

Aristotle, *On Sophistical Refutations*, tr. W. A. Pickard, selections

Section 1

Part 1

Let us now discuss sophistic refutations, i.e. what appear to be refutations but are really fallacies instead. We will begin in the natural order with the first.

That some reasonings are genuine, while others seem to be so but are not, is evident. This happens with arguments, as also elsewhere, through a certain likeness between the genuine and the sham. For physically some people are in a vigorous condition, while others merely seem to be so by blowing and rigging themselves out as the tribesmen do their victims for sacrifice; and some people are beautiful thanks to their beauty, while others seem to be so, by dint of embellishing themselves. So it is, too, with inanimate things; for of these, too, some are really silver and others gold, while others are not and merely seem to be such to our sense; e.g. things made of litharge and tin seem to be of silver, while those made of yellow metal look golden. In the same way both reasoning and refutation are sometimes genuine, sometimes not, though inexperience may make them appear so: for inexperienced people obtain only, as it were, a distant view of these things. For reasoning rests on certain statements such that they involve necessarily the assertion of something other than what has been stated, through what has been stated: refutation is reasoning involving the contradictory of the given conclusion. Now some of them do not really achieve this, though they seem to do so for a number of reasons; and of these the most prolific and usual domain is the argument that turns upon names only. It is impossible in a discussion to bring in the actual things discussed:

73

we use their names as symbols instead of them; and therefore we suppose that what follows in the names, follows in the things as well, just as people who calculate suppose in regard to their counters. But the two cases (names and things) are not alike. For names are finite and so is the sum-total of formulae, while things are infinite in number. Inevitably, then, the same formulae, and a single name, have a number of meanings. Accordingly just as, in counting, those who are not clever in manipulating their counters are taken in by the experts, in the same way in arguments too those who are not well acquainted with the force of names misreason both in their own discussions and when they listen to others. For this reason, then, and for others to be mentioned later, there exists both reasoning and refutation that is apparent but not real. Now for some people it is better worth while to seem to be wise, than to be wise without seeming to be (for the art of the sophist is the semblance of wisdom without the reality, and the sophist is one who makes money from an apparent but unreal wisdom); for them, then, it is clearly essential also to seem to accomplish the task of a wise man rather than to accomplish it without seeming to do so. To reduce it to a single point of contrast it is the business of one who knows a thing, himself to avoid fallacies in the subjects which he knows and to be able to show up the man who makes them; and of these accomplishments the one depends on the faculty to render an answer, and the other upon the securing of one. Those, then, who would be sophists are bound to study the class of arguments aforesaid: for it is worth their while: for a faculty of this kind will make a man seem to be wise, and this is the purpose they happen to have in view.

Clearly, then, there exists a class of arguments of this kind, and it is at this kind of ability that those aim whom we call sophists. Let us now go on to discuss how many kinds there are of sophistical arguments, and how many in number are the elements of which this faculty is composed, and how many branches there happen to be of this inquiry, and the other factors that contribute to this art.

Part 2

Of arguments in dialogue form there are four classes:
Didactic, Dialectical, Examination-arguments, and Contentious
arguments. Didactic arguments are those that reason from the
principles appropriate to each subject and not from the opinions
held by the answerer (for the learner should take things on trust):
dialectical arguments are those that reason from premisses
generally accepted, to the contradictory of a given thesis:
examination-arguments are those that reason from premisses
which are accepted by the answerer and which any one who
pretends to possess knowledge of the subject is bound to know-in
what manner, has been defined in another treatise: contentious
arguments are those that reason or appear to reason to a
conclusion from premisses that appear to be generally accepted
but are not so. The subject, then, of demonstrative arguments has
been discussed in the Analytics, while that of dialectic arguments
and examination-arguments has been discussed elsewhere: let us
now proceed to speak of the arguments used in competitions and
contests.

Part 3

First we must grasp the number of aims entertained by those who
argue as competitors and rivals to the death. These are five in
number, refutation, fallacy, paradox, solecism, and fifthly to
reduce the opponent in the discussion to babbling-i.e. to constrain
him to repeat himself a number of times: or it is to produce the
appearance of each of these things without the reality. For they
choose if possible plainly to refute the other party, or as the
second best to show that he is committing some fallacy, or as a
third best to lead him into paradox, or fourthly to reduce him to
solecism, i.e. to make the answerer, in consequence of the
argument, to use an ungrammatical expression; or, as a last resort,
to make him repeat himself.

Part 4

There are two styles of refutation: for some depend on the language used, while some are independent of language. Those ways of producing the false appearance of an argument which depend on language are six in number: they are ambiguity, amphiboly, combination, division of words, accent, form of expression. Of this we may assure ourselves both by induction, and by syllogistic proof based on this-and it may be on other assumptions as well-that this is the number of ways in which we might fall to mean the same thing by the same names or expressions. Arguments such as the following depend upon ambiguity. 'Those learn who know: for it is those who know their letters who learn the letters dictated to them'. For to 'learn' is ambiguous; it signifies both 'to understand' by the use of knowledge, and also 'to acquire knowledge'. Again, 'Evils are good: for what needs to be is good, and evils must needs be'. For 'what needs to be' has a double meaning: it means what is inevitable, as often is the case with evils, too (for evil of some kind is inevitable), while on the other hand we say of good things as well that they 'need to be'. Moreover, 'The same man is both seated and standing and he is both sick and in health: for it is he who stood up who is standing, and he who is recovering who is in health: but it is the seated man who stood up, and the sick man who was recovering'. For 'The sick man does so and so', or 'has so and so done to him' is not single in meaning: sometimes it means 'the man who is sick or is seated now', sometimes 'the man who was sick formerly'. Of course, the man who was recovering was the sick man, who really was sick at the time: but the man who is in health is not sick at the same time: he is 'the sick man' in the sense not that he is sick now, but that he was sick formerly. Examples such as the following depend upon amphiboly: 'I wish that you the enemy may capture'. Also the thesis, 'There must be knowledge of what one knows': for it is possible by this phrase to mean that knowledge belongs to both the knower and the known. Also, 'There must be sight of what one sees: one sees the pillar:

76

ergo the pillar has sight'. Also, 'What you profess to-be, that you profess to-be: you profess a stone to-be: ergo you profess-to-be a stone'. Also, 'Speaking of the silent is possible': for 'speaking of the silent' also has a double meaning: it may mean that the speaker is silent or that the things of which he speaks are so. There are three varieties of these ambiguities and amphibolies: (1) When either the expression or the name has strictly more than one meaning, e.g. aetos and the 'dog'; (2) when by custom we use them so; (3) when words that have a simple sense taken alone have more than one meaning in combination; e.g. 'knowing letters'. For each word, both 'knowing' and 'letters', possibly has a single meaning: but both together have more than one-either that the letters themselves have knowledge or that someone else has it of them.

Amphiboly and ambiguity, then, depend on these modes of speech. Upon the combination of words there depend instances such as the following: 'A man can walk while sitting, and can write while not writing'. For the meaning is not the same if one divides the words and if one combines them in saying that 'it is possible to walk-while-sitting' and write while not writing]. The same applies to the latter phrase, too, if one combines the words 'to write-while-not-writing': for then it means that he has the power to write and not to write at once; whereas if one does not combine them, it means that when he is not writing he has the power to write. Also, 'He now if he has learnt his letters'. Moreover, there is the saying that 'One single thing if you can carry a crowd you can carry too'.

Upon division depend the propositions that 5 is 2 and 3, and odd, and that the greater is equal: for it is that amount and more besides. For the same phrase would not be thought always to have the same meaning when divided and when combined, e.g. 'I made thee a slave once a free man', and 'God-like Achilles left fifty a hundred men'.

An argument depending upon accent it is not easy to construct in unwritten discussion; in written discussions and in poetry it is easier. Thus (e.g.) some people emend Homer against those who criticize as unnatural his expression to men ou kataputhetai ombro. For they solve the difficulty by a change of accent, pronouncing the ou with an acuter accent. Also, in the passage about Agamemnon's dream, they say that Zeus did not himself say 'We grant him the fulfilment of his prayer', but that he bade the dream grant it. Instances such as these, then, turn upon the accentuation.

Others come about owing to the form of expression used, when what is really different is expressed in the same form, e.g. a masculine thing by a feminine termination, or a feminine thing by a masculine, or a neuter by either a masculine or a feminine; or, again, when a quality is expressed by a termination proper to quantity or vice versa, or what is active by a passive word, or a state by an active word, and so forth with the other divisions previously' laid down. For it is possible to use an expression to denote what does not belong to the class of actions at all as though it did so belong. Thus (e.g.) 'flourishing' is a word which in the form of its expression is like 'cutting' or 'building': yet the one denotes a certain quality-i.e. a certain condition-while the other denotes a certain action. In the same manner also in the other instances.

Refutations, then, that depend upon language are drawn from these common-place rules. Of fallacies, on the other hand, that are independent of language there are seven kinds:

(1) that which depends upon Accident:
(2) the use of an expression absolutely or not absolutely but with some qualification of respect or place, or time, or relation:

(3) that which depends upon ignorance of what 'refutation' is:
(4) that which depends upon the consequent:

(5) that which depends upon assuming the original conclusion:

(6) stating as cause what is not the cause:

(7) the making of more than one question into one.

Part 5

Fallacies, then, that depend on Accident occur whenever any attribute is claimed to belong in like manner to a thing and to its accident. For since the same thing has many accidents there is no necessity that all the same attributes should belong to all of a thing's predicates and to their subject as well. Thus (e.g.), 'If Coriscus be different from "man", he is different from himself: for he is a man': or 'If he be different from Socrates, and Socrates be a man, then', they say, 'he has admitted that Coriscus is different from a man, because it so happens (accidit) that the person from whom he said that he (Coriscus) is different is a man'.

Those that depend on whether an expression is used absolutely or in a certain respect and not strictly, occur whenever an expression used in a particular sense is taken as though it were used absolutely, e.g. in the argument 'If what is not is the object of an opinion, then what is not is': for it is not the same thing 'to be x' and 'to be' absolutely. Or again, 'What is, is not, if it is not a particular kind of being, e.g. if it is not a man.' For it is not the same thing 'not to be x' and 'not to be' at all: it looks as if it were, because of the closeness of the expression, i.e. because 'to be x' is but little different from 'to be', and 'not to be x' from 'not to be'. Likewise also with any argument that turns upon the point whether an expression is used in a certain respect or used absolutely. Thus e.g. 'Suppose an Indian to be black all over, but white in respect of his teeth; then he is both white and not white.' Or if both characters belong in a particular respect, then, they say, 'contrary attributes belong at the same time'. This kind of thing is in some cases easily seen by any one, e.g. suppose a man were to secure the statement that the Ethiopian is black, and were then to ask whether he is white in respect of his teeth; and then, if he be white in that respect, were to suppose at the conclusion of his questions that therefore he had proved dialectically that he was both white and not white. But in some cases it often passes undetected, viz. in all cases where, whenever a statement is made of something in a certain respect, it would be generally thought that the absolute statement follows as well; and also in all cases where it is not easy to see which of the attributes ought to be rendered strictly. A situation of this kind arises, where both the opposite attributes belong alike: for then there is general support for the view that one must agree absolutely to the assertion of both, or of neither: e.g. if a thing is half white and half black, is it white or black?

Other fallacies occur because the terms 'proof' or 'refutation' have not been defined, and because something is left out in their definition. For to refute is to contradict one and the same attribute-not merely the name, but the reality-and a name that is not merely synonymous but the same name-and to confute it from the propositions granted, necessarily, without including in the reckoning the original point to be proved, in the same respect and relation and manner and time in which it was asserted. A 'false assertion' about anything has to be defined in the same way. Some people, however, omit some one of the said conditions and give a merely apparent refutation, showing (e.g.) that the same thing is both double and not double: for two is double of one, but not double of three. Or, it may be, they show that it is both double and not double of the same thing, but not that it is so in the same respect: for it is double in length but not double in breadth. Or, it may be, they show it to be both double and not double of the same thing and in the same respect and manner, but not that it is so at the same time: and therefore their refutation is merely apparent. One might, with some violence, bring this fallacy into the group of fallacies dependent on language as well.

Those that depend on the assumption of the original point to be proved, occur in the same way, and in as many ways, as it is possible to beg the original point; they appear to refute because men lack the power to keep their eyes at once upon what is the same and what is different.

The refutation which depends upon the consequent arises because people suppose that the relation of consequence is convertible. For whenever, suppose A is, B necessarily is, they then suppose also that if B is, A necessarily is. This is also the source of the deceptions that attend opinions based on sense-perception. For people often suppose bile to be honey because honey is attended by a yellow colour: also, since after rain the ground is wet in consequence, we suppose that if the ground is wet, it has been raining; whereas that does not necessarily follow. In rhetoric proofs from signs are based on consequences. For when rhetoricians wish to show that a man is an adulterer, they take hold of some consequence of an adulterous life, viz. that the man is smartly dressed, or that he is observed to wander about at night. There are, however, many people of whom these things are true, while the charge in question is untrue. It happens like this also in real reasoning; e.g. Melissus' argument, that the universe is eternal, assumes that the universe has not come to be (for from what is not nothing could possibly come to be) and that what has come to be has done so from a first beginning. If, therefore, the universe has not come to be, it has no first beginning, and is therefore eternal. But this does not necessarily follow: for even if what has come to be always has a first beginning, it does not also follow that what has a first beginning has come to be; any more than it follows that if a man in a fever be hot, a man who is hot must be in a fever.

The refutation which depends upon treating as cause what is not a cause, occurs whenever what is not a cause is inserted in the argument, as though the refutation depended upon it. This kind of thing happens in arguments that reason ad impossible: for in these we are bound to demolish one of the premisses. If, then, the false cause be reckoned in among the questions that are necessary to establish the resulting impossibility, it will often be thought that the refutation depends upon it, e.g. in the proof that the 'soul' and 'life' are not the same: for if coming-to-be be contrary to perishing, then a particular form of perishing will have a particular form of coming-to-be as its contrary: now death is a particular form of perishing and is contrary to life: life, therefore, is a coming to-be, and to live is to come-to-be. But this is impossible: accordingly, the 'soul' and 'life' are not the same. Now this is not proved: for the impossibility results all the same, even if one does not say that life is the same as the soul, but merely says that life is contrary to death, which is a form of perishing, and that perishing has 'coming-to-be' as its contrary. Arguments of that kind, then, though not inconclusive absolutely, are inconclusive in relation to the proposed conclusion. Also even the questioners themselves often fail quite as much to see a point of that kind.

Such, then, are the arguments that depend upon the consequent and upon false cause. Those that depend upon the making of two questions into one occur whenever the plurality is undetected and a single answer is returned as if to a single question. Now, in some cases, it is easy to see that there is more than one, and that an answer is not to be given, e.g. 'Does the earth consist of sea, or the sky?' But in some cases it is less easy, and then people treat the question as one, and either confess their defeat by failing to answer the question, or are exposed to an apparent refutation. Thus 'Is A and is B a man?' 'Yes.' 'Then if any one hits A and B, he will strike a man' (singular),'not men' (plural). Or again, where part is good and part bad, 'is the whole good or bad?' For whichever he says, it is possible that he might be thought to expose himself to an apparent refutation or to make an apparently false statement: for to say that something is good which is not good, or not good which is good, is to make a false statement. Sometimes, however, additional premisses may actually give rise to a genuine refutation; e.g. suppose a man were to grant that the descriptions 'white' and 'naked' and 'blind' apply to one thing and to a number of things in a like sense. For if 'blind' describes a thing that cannot see though nature designed it to see, it will also describe things that cannot see though nature designed them to do so. Whenever, then, one thing can see while another cannot, they will either both be able to see or else both be blind; which is impossible.

Part 6

The right way, then, is either to divide apparent proofs and refutations as above, or else to refer them all to ignorance of what 'refutation' is, and make that our starting-point: for it is possible to analyse all the aforesaid modes of fallacy into breaches of the definition of a refutation. In the first place, we may see if they are inconclusive: for the conclusion ought to result from the premisses laid down, so as to compel us necessarily to state it and not merely to seem to compel us. Next we should also take the definition bit by bit, and try the fallacy thereby. For of the fallacies that consist in language, some depend upon a double meaning, e.g. ambiguity of words and of phrases, and the fallacy of like verbal forms (for we habitually speak of everything as though it were a particular substance)-while fallacies of combination and division and accent arise because the phrase in question or the term as altered is not the same as was intended. Even this, however, should be the same, just as the thing signified should be as well, if a refutation or proof is to be effected; e.g. if the point concerns a doublet, then you should draw the conclusion of a 'doublet', not of a 'cloak'. For the former conclusion also would be true, but it has not been proved; we need a further question to show that 'doublet' means the same thing, in order to satisfy any one who asks why you think your point proved.

Fallacies that depend on Accident are clear cases of ignoratio elenchi when once 'proof' has been defined. For the same definition ought to hold good of 'refutation' too, except that a mention of 'the contradictory' is here added: for a refutation is a proof of the contradictory. If, then, there is no proof as regards an accident of anything, there is no refutation. For supposing, when A and B are, C must necessarily be, and C is white, there is no necessity for it to be white on account of the syllogism. So, if the triangle has its angles equal to two right-angles, and it happens to be a figure, or the simplest element or starting point, it is not because it is a figure or a starting point or simplest element that it has this character. For the demonstration proves the point about it not qua figure or qua simplest element, but qua triangle. Likewise also in other cases. If, then, refutation is a proof, an argument which argued per accidens could not be a refutation. It is, however, just in this that the experts and men of science generally suffer refutation at the hand of the unscientific: for the latter meet the scientists with reasonings constituted per accidens; and the scientists for lack of the power to draw distinctions either say 'Yes' to their questions, or else people suppose them to have said 'Yes', although they have not.

Those that depend upon whether something is said in a certain respect only or said absolutely, are clear cases of ignoratio elenchi because the affirmation and the denial are not concerned with the same point. For of 'white in a certain respect' the negation is 'not white in a certain respect', while of 'white absolutely' it is 'not white, absolutely'. If, then, a man treats the admission that a thing is 'white in a certain respect' as though it were said to be white absolutely, he does not effect a refutation, but merely appears to do so owing to ignorance of what refutation is.

The clearest cases of all, however, are those that were previously described' as depending upon the definition of a 'refutation': and this is also why they were called by that name. For the appearance of a refutation is produced because of the omission in the definition, and if we divide fallacies in the above manner, we ought to set 'Defective definition' as a common mark upon them all.

Those that depend upon the assumption of the original point and upon stating as the cause what is not the cause, are clearly shown to be cases of ignoratio elenchi through the definition thereof. For the conclusion ought to come about 'because these things are so', and this does not happen where the premisses are not causes of it: and again it should come about without taking into account the original point, and this is not the case with those arguments which depend upon begging the original point.

Those that depend upon the assumption of the original point and upon stating as the cause what is not the cause, are clearly shown to be cases of ignoratio elenchi through the definition thereof. For the conclusion ought to come about 'because these things are so', and this does not happen where the premisses are not causes of it: and again it should come about without taking into account the original point, and this is not the case with those arguments which depend upon begging the original point.

Those that depend upon the consequent are a branch of Accident: for the consequent is an accident, only it differs from the accident in this, that you may secure an admission of the accident in the case of one thing only (e.g. the identity of a yellow thing and honey and of a white thing and swan), whereas the consequent always involves more than one thing: for we claim that things that are the same as one and the same thing are also the same as one another, and this is the ground of a refutation dependent on the consequent. It is, however, not always true, e.g. suppose that and B are the same as C per accidens; for both 'snow' and the 'swan' are the same as something white'. Or again, as in Melissus' argument, a man assumes that to 'have been generated' and to 'have a beginning' are the same thing, or to 'become equal' and to 'assume the same magnitude'. For because what has been generated has a beginning, he claims also that what has a beginning has been generated, and argues as though both what has been generated and what is finite were the same because each has a beginning. Likewise also in the case of things that are made equal he assumes that if things that assume one and the same magnitude become equal, then also things that become equal assume one magnitude: i.e. he assumes the consequent. Inasmuch, then, as a refutation depending on accident consists in ignorance of what a refutation is, clearly so also does a refutation depending on the consequent. We shall have further to examine this in another way as well.

Those fallacies that depend upon the making of several questions into one consist in our failure to dissect the definition of 'proposition'. For a proposition is a single statement about a single thing. For the same definition applies to 'one single thing only' and to the 'thing', simply, e.g. to 'man' and to 'one single man only' and likewise also in other cases. If, then, a 'single proposition' be one which claims a single thing of a single thing, a 'proposition', simply, will also be the putting of a question of that kind. Now since a proof starts from propositions and refutation is a proof, refutation, too, will start from propositions. If, then, a proposition is a single statement about a single thing, it is obvious that this fallacy too consists in ignorance of what a refutation is: for in it what is not a proposition appears to be one. If, then, the answerer has returned an answer as though to a single question, there will be a refutation; while if he has returned one not really but apparently, there will be an apparent refutation of his thesis. All the types of fallacy, then, fall under ignorance of what a refutation is, some of them because the contradiction, which is the distinctive mark of a refutation, is merely apparent, and the rest failing to conform to the definition of a proof.

...

Part 12

So much, then, for apparent refutations. As for showing that the answerer is committing some fallacy, and drawing his argument into paradox-for this was the second item of the sophist's programme-in the first place, then, this is best brought about by a certain manner of questioning and through the question. For to put the question without framing it with reference to any definite subject is a good bait for these purposes: for people are more inclined to make mistakes when they talk at large, and they talk at large when they have no definite subject before them. Also the putting of several questions, even though the position against which one is arguing be quite definite, and the claim that he shall say only what he thinks, create abundant opportunity for drawing him into paradox or fallacy, and also, whether to any of these questions he replies 'Yes' or replies 'No', of leading him on to statements against which one is well off for a line of attack. Nowadays, however, men are less able to play foul by these means than they were formerly: for people rejoin with the question, 'What has that to do with the original subject?' It is, too, an elementary rule for eliciting some fallacy or paradox that one should never put a controversial question straight away, but say that one puts it from the wish for information: for the process of inquiry thus invited gives room for an attack.

A rule specially appropriate for showing up a fallacy is the sophistic rule, that one should draw the answerer on to the kind of statements against which one is well supplied with arguments: this can be done both properly and improperly, as was said before.' Again, to draw a paradoxical statement, look and see to what school of philosophers the person arguing with you belongs, and then question him as to some point wherein their doctrine is paradoxical to most people: for with every school there is some point of that kind. It is an elementary rule in these matters to have a collection of the special 'theses' of the various schools among your propositions. The solution recommended as appropriate here, too, is to point out that the paradox does not come about because of the argument: whereas this is what his opponent always really wants.

Moreover, argue from men's wishes and their professed opinions. For people do not wish the same things as they say they wish: they say what will look best, whereas they wish what appears to be to their interest: e.g. they say that a man ought to die nobly rather than to live in pleasure, and to live in honest poverty rather than in dishonourable riches; but they wish the opposite. Accordingly, a man who speaks according to his wishes must be led into stating the professed opinions of people, while he who speaks according to these must be led into admitting those that people keep hidden away: for in either case they are bound to introduce a paradox; for they will speak contrary either to men's professed or to their hidden opinions.

The widest range of common-place argument for leading men into paradoxical statement is that which depends on the standards of Nature and of the Law: it is so that both Callicles is drawn as arguing in the Gorgias, and that all the men of old supposed the result to come about: for nature (they said) and law are opposites, and justice is a fine thing by a legal standard, but not by that of nature. Accordingly, they said, the man whose statement agrees with the standard of nature you should meet by the standard of the law, but the man who agrees with the law by leading him to the facts of nature: for in both ways paradoxical statements may be committed. In their view the standard of nature was the truth, while that of the law was the opinion held by the majority. So that it is clear that they, too, used to try either to refute the answerer or to make him make paradoxical statements, just as the men of to-day do as well.

Some questions are such that in both forms the answer is paradoxical; e.g. 'Ought one to obey the wise or one's father?' and 'Ought one to do what is expedient or what is just?' and 'Is it preferable to suffer injustice or to do an injury?' You should lead people, then, into views opposite to the majority and to the philosophers; if any one speaks as do the expert reasoners, lead him into opposition to the majority, while if he speaks as do the majority, then into opposition to the reasoners. For some say that of necessity the happy man is just, whereas it is paradoxical to the many that a king should be happy. To lead a man into paradoxes of this sort is the same as to lead him into the opposition of the standards of nature and law: for the law represents the opinion of the majority, whereas philosophers speak according to the standard of nature and the truth.

Part 13

Paradoxes, then, you should seek to elicit by means of these common-place rules. Now as for making any one babble, we have already said what we mean by 'to babble'. This is the object in view in all arguments of the following kind: If it is all the same to state a term and to state its definition, the 'double' and 'double of half' are the same: if then 'double' be the 'double of half', it will be the 'double of half of half'. And if, instead of 'double', 'double of half' be again put, then the same expression will be repeated three times, 'double of half of half of half'. Also 'desire is of the pleasant, isn't it?' desire is conation for the pleasant: accordingly, 'desire' is 'conation for the pleasant for the pleasant'.

All arguments of this kind occur in dealing (1) with any relative terms which not only have relative genera, but are also themselves relative, and are rendered in relation to one and the same thing, as e.g. conation is conation for something, and desire is desire of something, and double is double of something, i.e. double of half: also in dealing (2) with any terms which, though they be not relative terms at all, yet have their substance, viz. the things of which they are the states or affections or what not, indicated as well in their definition, they being predicated of these things. Thus e.g. 'odd' is a 'number containing a middle': but there is an 'odd number': therefore there is a 'number-containing-a-middle number'. Also, if snubness be a concavity of the nose, and there be a snub nose, there is therefore a 'concave-nose nose'.

People sometimes appear to produce this result, without really producing it, because they do not add the question whether the expression 'double', just by itself, has any meaning or no, and if so, whether it has the same meaning, or a different one; but they draw their conclusion straight away. Still it seems, inasmuch as the word is the same, to have the same meaning as well.

Part 14

We have said before what kind of thing 'solecism' is.' It is possible both to commit it, and to seem to do so without doing so, and to do so without seeming to do so. Suppose, as Protagoras used to say that menis ('wrath') and pelex ('helmet') are masculine: according to him a man who calls wrath a 'destructress' (oulomenen) commits a solecism, though he does not seem to do so to other people, where he who calls it a 'destructor' (oulomenon) commits no solecism though he seems to do so. It is clear, then, that any one could produce this effect by art as well: and for this reason many arguments seem to lead to solecism which do not really do so, as happens in the case of refutations.

Almost all apparent solecisms depend upon the word 'this' (tode), and upon occasions when the inflection denotes neither a masculine nor a feminine object but a neuter. For 'he' (outos) signifies a masculine, and 'she' (aute) feminine; but 'this' (touto), though meant to signify a neuter, often also signifies one or other of the former: e.g. 'What is this?' 'It is Calliope'; 'it is a log'; 'it is Coriscus'. Now in the masculine and feminine the inflections are all different, whereas in the neuter some are and some are not. Often, then, when 'this' (touto) has been granted, people reason as if 'him' (touton) had been said: and likewise also they substitute one inflection for another. The fallacy comes about because 'this' (touto) is a common form of several inflections: for 'this' signifies sometimes 'he' (outos) and sometimes 'him' (touton). It should signify them alternately; when combined with 'is' (esti) it should be 'he', while with 'being' it should be 'him': e.g. 'Coriscus (Kopiskos) is', but 'being Coriscus' (Kopiskon). It happens in the same way in the case of feminine nouns as well, and in the case of the so-called 'chattels' that have feminine or masculine designations. For only those names which end in o and n, have the designation proper to a chattel, e.g. xulon ('log'), schoinion ('rope'); those which do not end so have that of a masculine or feminine object, though some of them we apply to chattels: e.g. askos ('wineskin') is a masculine noun, and kline ('bed') a feminine. For this reason in cases of this kind as well there will be a difference of the same sort between a construction with 'is' (esti) or with 'being' (to einai). Also, Solecism resembles in a certain way those refutations which are said to depend on the like expression of unlike things. For, just as there we come upon a material solecism, so here we come upon a verbal: for 'man' is both a 'matter' for expression and also a 'word': and so is white'.

It is clear, then, that for solecisms we must try to construct our argument out of the aforesaid inflections.

These, then, are the types of contentious arguments, and the subdivisions of those types, and the methods for conducting them aforesaid. But it makes no little difference if the materials for putting the question be arranged in a certain manner with a view to concealment, as in the case of dialectics. Following then upon what we have said, this must be discussed first.

Part 15

With a view then to refutation, one resource is length-for it is difficult to keep several things in view at once; and to secure length the elementary rules that have been stated before' should be employed. One resource, on the other hand, is speed; for when people are left behind they look ahead less. Moreover, there is anger and contentiousness, for when agitated everybody is less able to take care of himself. Elementary rules for producing anger are to make a show of the wish to play foul, and to be altogether shameless. Moreover, there is the putting of one's questions alternately, whether one has more than one argument leading to the same conclusion, or whether one has arguments to show both that something is so, and that it is not so: for the result is that he has to be on his guard at the same time either against more than one line, or against contrary lines, of argument. In general, all the methods described before of producing concealment are useful also for purposes of contentious argument: for the object of concealment is to avoid detection, and the object of this is to deceive.

To counter those who refuse to grant whatever they suppose to help one's argument, one should put the question negatively, as though desirous of the opposite answer, or at any rate as though one put the question without prejudice; for when it is obscure what answer one wants to secure, people are less refractory. Also when, in dealing with particulars, a man grants the individual case, when the induction is done you should often not put the universal as a question, but take it for granted and use it: for sometimes people themselves suppose that they have granted it, and also appear to the audience to have done so, for they remember the induction and assume that the questions could not have been put for nothing. In cases where there is no term to indicate the universal, still you should avail yourself of the resemblance of the particulars to suit your purpose; for resemblance often escapes detection. Also, with a view to obtaining your premiss, you ought to put it in your question side by side with its contrary. E.g. if it were necessary to secure the admission that 'A man should obey his father in everything', ask 'Should a man obey his parents in everything, or disobey them in everything?'; and to secure that 'A number multiplied by a large number is a large number', ask 'Should one agree that it is a large number or a small one?' For then, if compelled to choose, one will be more inclined to think it a large one: for the placing of their contraries close beside them makes things look big to men, both relatively and absolutely, and worse and better.

A strong appearance of having been refuted is often produced by the most highly sophistical of all the unfair tricks of questioners, when without proving anything, instead of putting their final proposition as a question, they state it as a conclusion, as though they had proved that 'Therefore so-and-so is not true'

It is also a sophistical trick, when a paradox has been laid down, first to propose at the start some view that is generally accepted, and then claim that the answerer shall answer what he thinks about it, and to put one's question on matters of that kind in the form 'Do you think that...?' For then, if the question be taken as one of the premisses of one's argument, either a refutation or a paradox is bound to result; if he grants the view, a refutation; if he refuses to grant it or even to admit it as the received opinion, a paradox; if he refuses to grant it, but admits that it is the received opinion, something very like a refutation, results.

Moreover, just as in rhetorical discourses, so also in those aimed at refutation, you should examine the discrepancies of the answerer's position either with his own statements, or with those of persons whom he admits to say and do aright, moreover with those of people who are generally supposed to bear that kind of character, or who are like them, or with those of the majority or of all men. Also just as answerers, too, often, when they are in process of being confuted, draw a distinction, if their confutation is just about to take place, so questioners also should resort to this from time to time to counter objectors, pointing out, supposing that against one sense of the words the objection holds, but not against the other, that they have taken it in the latter sense, as e.g. Cleophon does in the Mandrobulus. They should also break off their argument and cut down their other lines of attack, while in answering, if a man perceives this being done beforehand, he should put in his objection and have his say first. One should also lead attacks sometimes against positions other than the one stated, on the understood condition that one cannot find lines of attack against the view laid down, as Lycophron did when ordered to deliver a eulogy upon the lyre. To counter those who demand 'Against what are you directing your effort?', since one is generally thought bound to state the charge made, while, on the other hand, some ways of stating it make the defence too easy, you should state as your aim only the general result that always happens in refutations, namely the contradiction of his thesis -viz. that your effort is to deny what he has affirmed, or to affirm what he denied: don't say that you are trying to show that the knowledge of contraries is, or is not, the same. One must not ask one's conclusion in the form of a premiss, while some conclusions should not even be put as questions at all; one should take and use it as granted.

Part 16

We have now therefore dealt with the sources of questions, and the methods of questioning in contentious disputations: next we have to speak of answering, and of how solutions should be made, and of what requires them, and of what use is served by arguments of this kind.
The use of them, then, is, for philosophy, twofold. For in the first place, since for the most part they depend upon the expression, they put us in a better condition for seeing in how many senses any term is used, and what kind of resemblances and what kind of differences occur between things and between their names. In the second place they are useful for one's own personal researches; for the man who is easily committed to a fallacy by some one else, and does not perceive it, is likely to incur this fate of himself also on many occasions. Thirdly and lastly, they further contribute to one's reputation, viz. the reputation of being well trained in everything, and not inexperienced in anything: for that a party to arguments should find fault with them, if he cannot definitely

point out their weakness, creates a suspicion, making it seem as though it were not the truth of the matter but merely inexperience that put him out of temper.

Answerers may clearly see how to meet arguments of this kind, if our previous account was right of the sources whence fallacies came, and also our distinctions adequate of the forms of dishonesty in putting questions. But it is not the same thing take an argument in one's hand and then to see and solve its faults, as it is to be able to meet it quickly while being subjected to questions: for what we know, we often do not know in a different context. Moreover, just as in other things speed is enhanced by training, so it is with arguments too, so that supposing we are unpractised, even though a point be clear to us, we are often too late for the right moment. Sometimes too it happens as with diagrams; for there we can sometimes analyse the figure, but not construct it again: so too in refutations, though we know the thing on which the connexion of the argument depends, we still are at a loss to split the argument apart.

...

Part 24

In dealing with arguments that depend on Accident, one and the same solution meets all cases. For since it is indeterminate when an attribute should be ascribed to a thing, in cases where it belongs to the accident of the thing, and since in some cases it is generally agreed and people admit that it belongs, while in others they deny that it need belong, we should therefore, as soon as the conclusion has been drawn, say in answer to them all alike, that there is no need for such an attribute to belong. One must, however, be prepared to adduce an example of the kind of attribute meant. All arguments such as the following depend upon Accident. 'Do you know what I am going to ask you? you know the man who is approaching', or 'the man in the mask'? 'Is the statue your work of art?' or 'Is the dog your father?' 'Is the product of a small number with a small number a small number?' For it is evident in all these cases that there is no necessity for the attribute which is true of the thing's accident to be true of the thing as well. For only to things that are indistinguishable and one in essence is it generally agreed that all the same attributes belong; whereas in the case of a good thing, to be good is not the same as to be going to be the subject of a question; nor in the case of a man approaching, or wearing a mask, is 'to be approaching' the same thing as 'to be Coriscus', so that suppose I know Coriscus, but do not know the man who is approaching, it still isn't the case that I both know and do not know the same man; nor, again, if this is mine and is also a work of art, is it therefore my work of art, but my property or thing or something else. (The solution is after the same manner in the other cases as well.)

Some solve these refutations by demolishing the original proposition asked: for they say that it is possible to know and not to know the same thing, only not in the same respect: accordingly, when they don't know the man who is coming towards them, but do know Corsicus, they assert that they do know and don't know the same object, but not in the same respect. Yet, as we have already remarked, the correction of arguments that depend upon the same point ought to be the same, whereas this one will not stand if one adopts the same principle in regard not to knowing something, but to being, or to being is a in a certain state, e.g. suppose that X is father, and is also yours: for if in some cases this is true and it is possible to know and not to know the same thing, yet with that case the solution stated has nothing to do. Certainly there is nothing to prevent the same argument from having a number of flaws; but it is not the exposition of any and every fault that constitutes a solution: for it is possible for a man to show that a false conclusion has been proved, but not to show on what it depends, e.g. in the case of Zeno's argument to prove that motion is impossible. So that even if any one were to try to establish that this doctrine is an impossible one, he still is mistaken, and even if he proved his case ten thousand times over, still this is no solution of Zeno's argument: for the solution was all along an exposition of false reasoning, showing on what its falsity depends. If then he has not proved his case, or is trying to establish even a true proposition, or a false one, in a false manner, to point this out is a true solution. Possibly, indeed, the present suggestion may very well apply in some cases: but in these cases, at any rate, not even this would be generally agreed: for he knows both that Coriscus is Coriscus and that the approaching figure is approaching. To know and not to know the same thing is generally thought to be possible, when e.g. one knows that X is white, but does not realize that he is musical: for in that way he does know and not know the same thing, though not in the same respect. But as to the approaching figure and Coriscus he knows both that it is approaching and that he is Coriscus.

A like mistake to that of those whom we have mentioned is that of those who solve the proof that every number is a small number: for if, when the conclusion is not proved, they pass this over and say that a conclusion has been proved and is true, on the ground that every number is both great and small, they make a mistake.

Some people also use the principle of ambiguity to solve the aforesaid reasonings, e.g. the proof that 'X is your father', or 'son', or 'slave'. Yet it is evident that if the appearance a proof depends upon a plurality of meanings, the term, or the expression in question, ought to bear a number of literal senses, whereas no one speaks of A as being 'B's child' in the literal sense, if B is the child's master, but the combination depends upon Accident. 'Is A yours?' 'Yes.' 'And is A a child?' 'Yes.' 'Then the child A is yours,' because he happens to be both yours and a child; but he is not 'your child'.

There is also the proof that 'something "of evils" is good'; for wisdom is a 'knowledge "of evils"'. But the expression that this is 'of so and-so' (='so-and-so's') has not a number of meanings: it means that it is 'so-and-so's property'. We may suppose of course, on the other hand, that it has a number of meanings-for we also say that man is 'of the animals', though not their property; and also that any term related to 'evils' in a way expressed by a genitive case is on that account a so-and-so 'of evils', though it is not one of the evils-but in that case the apparently different meanings seem to depend on whether the term is used relatively or absolutely. 'Yet it is conceivably possible to find a real ambiguity in the phrase "Something of evils is good".' Perhaps, but not with regard to the phrase in question. It would occur more nearly, suppose that 'A servant is good of the wicked'; though perhaps it is not quite found even there: for a thing may be 'good' and be 'X's' without being at the same time 'X's good'. Nor is the saying that 'Man is of the animals' a phrase with a number of meanings: for a phrase does not become possessed of a number of meanings merely suppose we express it elliptically: for we express 'Give me the Iliad' by quoting half a line of it, e.g. 'Give me "Sing, goddess, of the wrath..."'

Part 25

Those arguments which depend upon an expression that is valid of a particular thing, or in a particular respect, or place, or manner, or relation, and not valid absolutely, should be solved by considering the conclusion in relation to its contradictory, to see if any of these things can possibly have happened to it. For it is impossible for contraries and opposites and an affirmative and a negative to belong to the same thing absolutely; there is, however, nothing to prevent each from belonging in a particular respect or relation or manner, or to prevent one of them from belonging in a particular respect and the other absolutely. So that if this one belongs absolutely and that one in a particular respect, there is as yet no refutation. This is a feature one has to find in the conclusion by examining it in comparison with its contradictory.

All arguments of the following kind have this feature: 'Is it possible for what is-not to be? "No." But, you see, it is something, despite its not being.' Likewise also, Being will not be; for it will not he some particular form of being. Is it possible for the same man at the same time to be a keeper and a breaker of his oath?' 'Can the same man at the same time both obey and disobey the same man?' Or isn't it the case that being something in particular and Being are not the same? On the other hand, Not-being, even if it be something, need not also have absolute 'being' as well. Nor if a man keeps his oath in this particular instance or in this particular respect, is he bound also to be a keeper of oaths absolutely, but he who swears that he will break his oath, and then breaks it, keeps this particular oath only; he is not a keeper of his oath: nor is the disobedient man 'obedient', though he obeys one particular command. The argument is similar, also, as regards the problem whether the same man can at the same time say what is both false and true: but it appears to be a troublesome question because it is not easy to see in which of the two connexions the word 'absolutely' is to be rendered-with 'true' or with 'false'. There is, however, nothing to prevent it from being false absolutely, though true in some particular respect or relation, i.e. being true in some things, though not 'true' absolutely. Likewise also in cases of some particular relation and place and time. For all arguments of the following kind depend upon this.' Is health, or wealth, a good thing?' 'Yes.' 'But to the fool who does not use it aright it is not a good thing: therefore it is both good and not good.' 'Is health, or political power, a good thing?' 'Yes. "But sometimes it is not particularly good: therefore the same thing is both good and not good to the same man.' Or rather there is nothing to prevent a thing, though good absolutely, being not good to a particular man, or being good to a particular man, and yet not good or here. 'Is that which the prudent man would not wish, an evil?' 'Yes.' 'But to get rid of, he would not wish the good: therefore the good is an evil.' But that is a mistake; for it is not the same thing to say 'The good is an evil' and 'to get rid of the good is an evil'. Likewise also the argument of the thief is mistaken. For it is not the case that if the thief is an evil thing, acquiring things is also evil: what he wishes, therefore, is not what is evil but what is good; for to acquire something good is good. Also, disease is an evil thing, but not to get rid of disease. 'Is the just preferable to the unjust, and what takes place justly to what takes place unjustly? 'Yes.' 'But to to be put to death unjustly is preferable.' 'Is it just that each should have his own?' 'Yes.' 'But whatever decisions a man comes to on the strength of his personal opinion, even if it be a false opinion, are valid in law: therefore the same result is both just and unjust.' Also, should one decide in favour of him who says what is unjust?' 'The former.' 'But you see, it is just for the injured party to say fully the things he has suffered; and these are fallacies. For because to suffer a thing unjustly is preferable, unjust ways are not therefore preferable, though in this particular case the unjust may very well be better than the just. Also, to have one's own is just, while to have what is another's is not just: all the same, the decision in question may very well be a just decision, whatever it be that the opinion of the man who gave the decision supports: for because it is just in this particular case or in this particular manner, it is not also just absolutely. Likewise also, though things are unjust, there is nothing to prevent the speaking of them being just: for because to speak of things is just, there is no necessity that the things should be just, any more than because to speak of things be of use, the things need be of use. Likewise also in the case of what is just. So that it is not the case that because the things spoken of are unjust, the victory goes to him who speaks unjust things: for he speaks of things that are just to speak of, though absolutely, i.e. to suffer, they are unjust.

Part 26

Refutations that depend on the definition of a refutation must, according to the plan sketched above, be met by comparing together the conclusion with its contradictory, and seeing that it shall involve the same attribute in the same respect and relation and manner and time. If this additional question be put at the start, you should not admit that it is impossible for the same thing to be both double and not double, but grant that it is possible, only not in such a way as was agreed to constitute a refutation of your case. All the following arguments depend upon a point of that kind. 'Does a man who knows A to be A, know the thing called A?' and in the same way, 'is one who is ignorant that A is A ignorant of the thing called A?' 'Yes.' 'But one who knows that Coriscus is Coriscus might be ignorant of the fact that he is musical, so that he both knows and is ignorant of the same thing.' Is a thing four cubits long greater than a thing three cubits long?' 'Yes.' 'But a thing might grow from three to four cubits in length; 'now what is 'greater' is greater than a 'less': accordingly the thing in question will be both greater and less than itself in the same respect.

Part 27

As to refutations that depend on begging and assuming the original point to be proved, suppose the nature of the question to be obvious, one should not grant it, even though it be a view generally held, but should tell him the truth. Suppose, however, that it escapes one, then, thanks to the badness of arguments of that kind, one should make one's error recoil upon the questioner, and say that he has brought no argument: for a refutation must be proved independently of the original point. Secondly, one should say that the point was granted under the impression that he intended not to use it as a premiss, but to reason against it, in the opposite way from that adopted in refutations on side issues.

Part 28

Also, those refutations that bring one to their conclusion through the consequent you should show up in the course of the argument itself. The mode in which consequences follow is twofold. For the argument either is that as the universal follows on its particular-as (e.g.) 'animal' follows from 'man'-so does the particular on its universal: for the claim is made that if A is always found with B, then B also is always found with A. Or else it proceeds by way of the opposites of the terms involved: for if A follows B, it is claimed that A's opposite will follow B's opposite. On this latter claim the argument of Melissus also depends: for he claims that because that which has come to be has a beginning, that which has not come to be has none, so that if the heaven has not come to be, it is also eternal. But that is not so; for the sequence is vice versa.

Part 29

In the case of any refutations whose reasoning depends on some addition, look and see if upon its subtraction the absurdity follows none the less: and then if so, the answerer should point this out, and say that he granted the addition not because he really thought it, but for the sake of the argument, whereas the questioner has not used it for the purpose of his argument at all.

Part 30

To meet those refutations which make several questions into one, one should draw a distinction between them straight away at the start. For a question must be single to which there is a single answer, so that one must not affirm or deny several things of one thing, nor one thing of many, but one of one. But just as in the case of ambiguous terms, an attribute belongs to a term sometimes in both its senses, and sometimes in neither, so that a simple answer does one, as it happens, no harm despite the fact that the question is not simple, so it is in these cases of double questions too. Whenever, then, the several attributes belong to the one subject, or the one to the many, the man who gives a simple answer encounters no obstacle even though he has committed this mistake: but whenever an attribute belongs to one subject but not to the other, or there is a question of a number of attributes belonging to a number of subjects and in one sense both belong to both, while in another sense, again, they do not, then there is trouble, so that one must beware of this. Thus (e.g.) in the following arguments: Supposing to be good and B evil, you will, if you give a single answer about both, be compelled to say that it is true to call these good, and that it is true to call them evil and likewise to call them neither good nor evil (for each of them has not each character), so that the same thing will be both good and evil and neither good nor evil. Also, since everything is the same as itself and different from anything else, inasmuch as the man who answers double questions simply can be made to say that several things are 'the same' not as other things but 'as themselves', and also that they are different from themselves, it follows that the same things must be both the same as and different from themselves. Moreover, if what is good becomes evil while what is evil is good, then they must both become two. So of two unequal things each being equal to itself, it will follow that they are both equal and unequal to themselves.

Now these refutations fall into the province of other solutions as well: for 'both' and 'all' have more than one meaning, so that the resulting affirmation and denial of the same thing does not occur, except verbally: and this is not what we meant by a refutation. But it is clear that if there be not put a single question on a number of points, but the answerer has affirmed or denied one attribute only of one subject only, the absurdity will not come to pass.

...

Part 33

We must also observe that of all the arguments aforesaid it is easier with some to see why and where the reasoning leads the hearer astray, while with others it is more difficult, though often they are the same arguments as the former. For we must call an argument the same if it depends upon the same point; but the same argument is apt to be thought by some to depend on diction, by others on accident, and by others on something else, because each of them, when worked with different terms, is not so clear as it was. Accordingly, just as in fallacies that depend on ambiguity, which are generally thought to be the silliest form of fallacy, some are clear even to the man in the street (for humorous phrases nearly all depend on diction; e.g. 'The man got the cart down from the stand'; and 'Where are you bound?' 'To the yard arm'; and 'Which cow will calve afore?' 'Neither, but both behind;' and 'Is the North wind clear?' 'No, indeed; for it has murdered the beggar and the merchant." Is he a Good enough-King?' 'No, indeed; a Rob-son': and so with the great majority of the rest as well), while others appear to elude the most expert (and it is a symptom of this that they often fight about their terms, e.g. whether the meaning of 'Being' and 'One' is the same in all their applications or different; for some think that 'Being' and 'One' mean the same; while others solve the argument of Zeno and Parmenides by asserting that 'One' and 'Being' are used in a number of senses), likewise also as regards fallacies of Accident and each of the other types, some of the arguments will be easier to see while others are more difficult; also to grasp to which class a fallacy belongs, and whether it is a refutation or not a refutation, is not equally easy in all cases.

An incisive argument is one which produces the greatest perplexity: for this is the one with the sharpest fang. Now perplexity is twofold, one which occurs in reasoned arguments, respecting which of the propositions asked one is to demolish, and the other in contentious arguments, respecting the manner in which one is to assent to what is propounded. Therefore it is in syllogistic arguments that the more incisive ones produce the keenest heart-searching. Now a syllogistic argument is most incisive if from premisses that are as generally accepted as possible it demolishes a conclusion that is accepted as generally as possible. For the one argument, if the contradictory is changed about, makes all the resulting syllogisms alike in character: for always from premisses that are generally accepted it will prove a conclusion, negative or positive as the case may be, that is just as generally accepted; and therefore one is bound to feel perplexed. An argument, then, of this kind is the most incisive, viz. the one that puts its conclusion on all fours with the propositions asked; and second comes the one that argues from premisses, all of which are equally convincing: for this will produce an equal perplexity as to what kind of premiss, of those asked, one should demolish. Herein is a difficulty: for one must demolish something, but what one must demolish is uncertain. Of contentious arguments, on the other hand, the most incisive is the one which, in the first place, is characterized by an initial uncertainty whether it has been properly reasoned or not; and also whether the solution depends on a false premiss or on the drawing of a distinction; while, of the rest, the second place is held by that whose solution clearly depends upon a distinction or a demolition, and yet it does not reveal clearly which it is of the premisses asked, whose demolition, or the drawing of a distinction within it, will bring the solution about, but even leaves it vague whether it is on the conclusion or on one of the premisses that the deception depends.

Now sometimes an argument which has not been properly reasoned is silly, supposing the assumptions required to be extremely contrary to the general view or false; but sometimes it ought not to be held in contempt. For whenever some question is left out, of the kind that concerns both the subject and the nerve of the argument, the reasoning that has both failed to secure this as well, and also failed to reason properly, is silly; but when what is omitted is some extraneous question, then it is by no means to be lightly despised, but the argument is quite respectable, though the questioner has not put his questions well.

Just as it is possible to bring a solution sometimes against the argument, at others against the questioner and his mode of questioning, and at others against neither of these, likewise also it is possible to marshal one's questions and reasoning both against the thesis, and against the answerer and against the time, whenever the solution requires a longer time to examine than the period available.

Part 34

As to the number, then, and kind of sources whence fallacies arise in discussion, and how we are to show that our opponent is committing a fallacy and make him utter paradoxes; moreover, by the use of what materials solescism is brought about, and how to question and what is the way to arrange the questions; moreover, as to the question what use is served by all arguments of this kind, and concerning the answerer's part, both as a whole in general, and in particular how to solve arguments and solecisms-on all these things let the foregoing discussion suffice. It remains to recall our original proposal and to bring our discussion to a close with a few words upon it.

Our programme was, then, to discover some faculty of reasoning about any theme put before us from the most generally accepted premises that there are. For that is the essential task of the art of discussion (dialectic) and of examination (peirastic). Inasmuch, however, as it is annexed to it, on account of the near presence of the art of sophistry (sophistic), not only to be able to conduct an examination dialectically but also with a show of knowledge, we therefore proposed for our treatise not only the aforesaid aim of being able to exact an account of any view, but also the aim of ensuring that in standing up to an argument we shall defend our thesis in the same manner by means of views as generally held as possible. The reason of this we have explained; for this, too, was why Socrates used to ask questions and not to answer them; for he used to confess that he did not know. We have made clear, in the course of what precedes, the number both of the points with reference to which, and of the materials from which, this will be accomplished, and also from what sources we can become well supplied with these: we have shown, moreover, how to question or arrange the questioning as a whole, and the problems concerning the answers and solutions to be used against the reasonings of the questioner. We have also cleared up the problems concerning all other matters that belong to the same inquiry into arguments. In addition to this we have been through the subject of Fallacies, as we have already stated above.

That our programme, then, has been adequately completed is clear. But we must not omit to notice what has happened in regard to this inquiry. For in the case of all discoveries the results of previous labours that have been handed down from others have been advanced bit by bit by those who have taken them on, whereas the original discoveries generally make advance that is small at first though much more useful than the development which later springs out of them. For it may be that in everything, as the saying is, 'the first start is the main part': and for this reason also it is the most difficult; for in proportion as it is most potent in its influence, so it is smallest in its compass and therefore most difficult to see: whereas when this is once discovered, it is easier to add and develop the remainder in connexion with it. This is in fact what has happened in regard to rhetorical speeches and to practically all the other arts: for those who discovered the beginnings of them advanced them in all only a little way, whereas the celebrities of to-day are the heirs (so to speak) of a long succession of men who have advanced them bit by bit, and so have developed them to their present form, Tisias coming next after the first founders, then Thrasymachus after Tisias, and Theodorus next to him, while several people have made their several contributions to it: and therefore it is not to be wondered at that the art has attained considerable dimensions. Of this inquiry, on the other hand, it was not the case that part of the work had been thoroughly done before, while part had not. Nothing existed at all. For the training given by the paid professors of contentious arguments was like the treatment of the matter by Gorgias. For they used to hand out speeches to be learned by heart, some rhetorical, others in the form of question and answer, each side supposing that their arguments on either side generally fall among them. And therefore the teaching they gave their pupils was ready but rough. For they used to suppose that they trained people by imparting to them not the art but its products, as though any one professing that he would impart a form of knowledge to obviate any pain in the feet, were then not to teach a man the art of shoe-making or the sources whence he can acquire anything of the kind, but were to present him with several kinds of shoes of all sorts: for he has helped him to meet his need, but has not imparted an art to him. Moreover, on the subject of Rhetoric there exists much that has been said long ago, whereas on the subject of reasoning we had nothing else of an earlier date to speak of at all, but were kept at work for a long time in experimental researches. If, then, it seems to you after inspection that, such being the situation as it existed at the start, our investigation is in a satisfactory condition compared with the other inquiries that have been developed by tradition, there must remain for all of you, or for our students, the task of extending us your pardon for the shortcomings of the inquiry, and for the discoveries thereof your warm thanks.

FALLACIES – NOTES

Fallacies of Language

Equivocation

Using a word with two different senses:
"Fire is god. Jim got fired. Therefore, Jim is god."

Amphiboly

Being unclear in syntax:
"Once I worshipped fire wearing a hat."

Accent

Being unclear in the stressed word:
"*We* didn't start the fire!" vs. "We didn't *start* the fire!" vs. "We didn't start the *fire!*"

Fallacies of Diversion

Attacking the Man (*ad hominem*)

Arguing against someone's personality instead of their argument:
"What do you mean fire is god? You're ugly."

Poisoning the Well

Pre-emptively attacking the supposed motivations of the argument:
"Whoever disagrees with the following is a traitor to the Persian empire: fire is god."

"You're Another" (*tu quoque*)

Accusing your opponent of the same mistake:
"Yes, I worship fire, but you're just as illogical as I am in worshipping water."

Genetic Fallacy

Attacks the supposed motivations of the argument:
"You only think fire is god because the Persian government told you so."

Appeal to Authority (*ad verecundiam*)
Quoting an irrelevant source as authoritative:
"Ben Affleck likes the Zoroastrian religion, so it must be true."

Appeal to Force (*ad baculum*)
Using violence to try to prove its point:
"If you don't agree with Zoroastrianism, you will be slapped in the face."

Appeal to Pity (*ad misericordiam*)
Confusing the sadness of something with a valid argument against it.
"I remember when the water-worshippers killed my father. It was devastating for me and my family. Therefore, fire is god."

Appeal to Shame (*ad ignominiam*)
Confusing the shamefulness of something with a valid argument against it.
"What do you mean you don't worship fire? Don't you realize that water-worshippers are a bunch of toothless rednecks?"

Appeal to Popularity (*ad populum*; "bandwagon fallacy")
Holding a view is correct only because many believe it:
"Everyone thinks that fire is god. It must be true."

Appeal to Ignorance (*ad ignorantiam*; "shifting the burden of proof")
Holding an implausible claim and asking the opponent to prove otherwise:
"Can you *prove* that fire is not, in fact, god?"

Fallacies of Oversimplification
Accident (*dicto simpliciter*)
Confusing substance with accident, or essence with qualification:
"Plato is different from Socrates. Socrates is a man. Therefore, Plato is not a man."

Composition and Division
Confusing a whole with a part:
"Each of the molecules in my body is microscopic. Therefore, my body is microscopic."

False Dilemma ("false dichotomy;" "The Black and White Fallacy")
Falsely limits the number of options:
"Either fire is god or water is god."

Fallacies of Argumentation
Non Sequitur ("does not follow")
Making any conclusion that is not necessary from the premises:
"My pants are green. Therefore, fire is god."

Circular Reasoning (*petitio principii*; "begging the question")
Assuming what you want to prove:
"Of course the Zoroastrian religion is true: all the Magi believe it and they're appointed by the fire god!"

Complex Question
Asking what appears to be one question which is in fact more than one:
"Have you finally admitted to yourself the truth that fire is god?"

Slippery Slope
Showing consequences to the argument that are not necessary or relevant:
"If we stop worshipping fire, the Persian empire will lose its identity, its people will be scattered, the Romans will attack us and we will all be destroyed."

Fallacies of Induction

Hasty Generalization

Making a conclusion with insufficient examples:

"Those four Persians believe that fire is god. Therefore, all Persians do."

False Cause (*post hoc ergo propter hoc*)

Claiming that something preceding something else must be its cause:

"I prayed to fire and my son got better. Therefore, the prayer healed my son."

Argument from Silence

Concluding that someone agrees or disagrees when they say nothing.

"I asked Jimmy if he believed in fire and he didn't say anything, so he must be an atheist."

"I asked Jimmy if he didn't believe in fire and he didn't say anything, so he must."

Selective Evidence

Only referring to the parts of the evidence that support your claim.

"Fire is god because it cannot be destroyed by wood, but rather destroys it" (ignoring the fact that it can be destroyed by water).

Fallacies of Procedure

Red Herring ("changing the subject")

Causing an irrelevant distraction to the argument:

"Look at how ugly those ice sculptures are. Fire must be god."

Straw Man

Setting up a false opponent; oversimplifying the opponent's position:

"So you think water is god just because it's wet? That's stupid."

JUDGMENT - TEXTS

Aristotle, *On Interpretation*, tr. E. M. Edghill

Section 1

Part 1

First we must define the terms 'noun' and 'verb', then the terms 'denial' and 'affirmation', then 'proposition' and 'sentence.'

Spoken words are the symbols of mental experience and written words are the symbols of spoken words. Just as all men have not the same writing, so all men have not the same speech sounds, but the mental experiences, which these directly symbolize, are the same for all, as also are those things of which our experiences are the images. This matter has, however, been discussed in my treatise about the soul, for it belongs to an investigation distinct from that which lies before us.

As there are in the mind thoughts which do not involve truth or falsity, and also those which must be either true or false, so it is in speech. For truth and falsity imply combination and separation. Nouns and verbs, provided nothing is added, are like thoughts without combination or separation; 'man' and 'white', as isolated terms, are not yet either true or false. In proof of this, consider the word 'goat-stag.' It has significance, but there is no truth or falsity about it, unless 'is' or 'is not' is added, either in the present or in some other tense.

113

Part 2

By a noun we mean a sound significant by convention, which has no reference to time, and of which no part is significant apart from the rest. In the noun 'Fairsteed,' the part 'steed' has no significance in and by itself, as in the phrase 'fair steed.' Yet there is a difference between simple and composite nouns; for in the former the part is in no way significant, in the latter it contributes to the meaning of the whole, although it has not an independent meaning. Thus in the word 'pirate-boat' the word 'boat' has no meaning except as part of the whole word.

The limitation 'by convention' was introduced because nothing is by nature a noun or name-it is only so when it becomes a symbol; inarticulate sounds, such as those which brutes produce, are significant, yet none of these constitutes a noun.

The expression 'not-man' is not a noun. There is indeed no recognized term by which we may denote such an expression, for it is not a sentence or a denial. Let it then be called an indefinite noun.

The expressions 'of Philo', 'to Philo', and so on, constitute not nouns, but cases of a noun. The definition of these cases of a noun is in other respects the same as that of the noun proper, but, when coupled with 'is', 'was', or will be', they do not, as they are, form a proposition either true or false, and this the noun proper always does, under these conditions. Take the words 'of Philo is' or 'of or 'of Philo is not'; these words do not, as they stand, form either a true or a false proposition.

Part 3

A verb is that which, in addition to its proper meaning, carries with it the notion of time. No part of it has any independent meaning, and it is a sign of something said of something else.

I will explain what I mean by saying that it carries with it the notion of time. 'Health' is a noun, but 'is healthy' is a verb; for besides its proper meaning it indicates the present existence of the state in question.

Moreover, a verb is always a sign of something said of something else, i.e. of something either predicable of or present in some other thing.

Such expressions as 'is not-healthy', 'is not, ill', I do not describe as verbs; for though they carry the additional note of time, and always form a predicate, there is no specified name for this variety; but let them be called indefinite verbs, since they apply equally well to that which exists and to that which does not.

Similarly 'he was healthy', 'he will be healthy', are not verbs, but tenses of a verb; the difference lies in the fact that the verb indicates present time, while the tenses of the verb indicate those times which lie outside the present.

Verbs in and by themselves are substantival and have significance, for he who uses such expressions arrests the hearer's mind, and fixes his attention; but they do not, as they stand, express any judgement, either positive or negative. For neither are 'to be' and 'not to be' the participle

115

'being' significant of any fact, unless something is added; for they do not themselves indicate anything, but imply a copulation, of which we cannot form a conception apart from the things coupled.

Part 4

A sentence is a significant portion of speech, some parts of which have an independent meaning, that is to say, as an utterance, though not as the expression of any positive judgement. Let me explain. The word 'human' has meaning, but does not constitute a proposition, either positive or negative. It is only when other words are added that the whole will form an affirmation or denial. But if we separate one syllable of the word 'human' from the other, it has no meaning; similarly in the word 'mouse', the part 'ouse' has no meaning in itself, but is merely a sound. In composite words, indeed, the parts contribute to the meaning of the whole; yet, as has been pointed out, they have not an independent meaning.

Every sentence has meaning, not as being the natural means by which a physical faculty is realized, but, as we have said, by convention. Yet every sentence is not a proposition; only such are propositions as have in them either truth or falsity. Thus a prayer is a sentence, but is neither true nor false.

Let us therefore dismiss all other types of sentence but the proposition, for this last concerns our present inquiry, whereas the investigation of the others belongs rather to the study of rhetoric or of poetry.

Part 5

The first class of simple propositions is the simple affirmation, the next, the simple denial; all others are only one by conjunction.

Every proposition must contain a verb or the tense of a verb. The phrase which defines the species 'man', if no verb in present, past, or future time be added, is not a proposition. It may be asked how the expression 'a footed animal with two feet' can be called single; for it is not the circumstance that the words follow in unbroken succession that effects the unity. This inquiry, however, finds its place in an investigation foreign to that before us.

We call those propositions single which indicate a single fact, or the conjunction of the parts of which results in unity: those propositions, on the other hand, are separate and many in number, which indicate many facts, or whose parts have no conjunction.

Let us, moreover, consent to call a noun or a verb an expression only, and not a proposition, since it is not possible for a man to speak in this way when he is expressing something, in such a way as to make a statement, whether his utterance is an answer to a question or an act of his own initiation.

To return: of propositions one kind is simple, i.e. that which asserts or denies something of something, the other composite, i.e. that which is compounded of simple propositions. A simple proposition is a statement, with meaning, as to the presence of something in a subject or its

.

absence, in the present, past, or future, according to the divisions of time.

Part 6

An affirmation is a positive assertion of something about something, a denial a negative assertion.

Now it is possible both to affirm and to deny the presence of something which is present or of something which is not, and since these same affirmations and denials are possible with reference to those times which lie outside the present, it would be possible to contradict any affirmation or denial. Thus it is plain that every affirmation has an opposite denial, and similarly every denial an opposite affirmation.

We will call such a pair of propositions a pair of contradictories. Those positive and negative propositions are said to be contradictory which have the same subject and predicate. The identity of subject and of predicate must not be 'equivocal'. Indeed there are definitive qualifications besides this, which we make to meet the casuistries of sophists.

Part 7

Some things are universal, others individual. By the term 'universal' I mean that which is of such a nature as to be predicated of many subjects, by 'individual' that which is not thus predicated. Thus 'man' is a universal, 'Callias' an individual.

Our propositions necessarily sometimes concern a universal subject, sometimes an individual.

If, then, a man states a positive and a negative proposition of universal character with regard to a universal, these two propositions are 'contrary'. By the expression 'a proposition of universal character with regard to a universal', such propositions as 'every man is white', 'no man is white' are meant. When, on the other hand, the positive and negative propositions, though they have regard to a universal, are yet not of universal character, they will not be contrary, albeit the meaning intended is sometimes contrary. As instances of propositions made with regard to a universal, but not of universal character, we may take the 'propositions 'man is white', 'man is not white'. 'Man' is a universal, but the proposition is not made as of universal character; for the word 'every' does not make the subject a universal, but rather gives the proposition a universal character. If, however, both predicate and subject are distributed, the proposition thus constituted is contrary to truth; no affirmation will, under such circumstances, be true. The proposition 'every man is every animal' is an example of this type.

An affirmation is opposed to a denial in the sense which I denote by the term 'contradictory', when, while the subject remains the same, the affirmation is of universal character and the denial is not. The affirmation 'every man is white' is the contradictory of the denial 'not every man is white', or again, the proposition 'no man is white' is the contradictory of the proposition 'some men are white'. But propositions are opposed as contraries when both the affirmation and the denial are universal, as in the sentences 'every man is white', 'no man is white', 'every man is just', 'no man is just'.

We see that in a pair of this sort both propositions cannot be true, but the contradictories of a pair of contraries can sometimes both be true with reference to the same subject; for instance 'not every man is white' and some men are white' are both true. Of such corresponding positive and negative propositions as refer to universals and have a universal character, one must be true and the other false. This is the case also when the reference is to individuals, as in the propositions 'Socrates is white', 'Socrates is not white'.

When, on the other hand, the reference is to universals, but the propositions are not universal, it is not always the case that one is true and the other false, for it is possible to state truly that man is white and that man is not white and that man is beautiful and that man is not beautiful; for if a man is deformed he is the reverse of beautiful, also if he is progressing towards beauty he is not yet beautiful.

This statement might seem at first sight to carry with it a contradiction, owing to the fact that the proposition 'man is not white' appears to be equivalent to the proposition 'no man is white'. This, however, is not the case, nor are they necessarily at the same time true or false.

It is evident also that the denial corresponding to a single affirmation is itself single; for the denial must deny just that which the affirmation affirms concerning the same subject, and must correspond with the affirmation both in the universal or particular character of the subject and in the distributed or undistributed sense in which it is understood.

For instance, the affirmation 'Socrates is white' has its proper denial in the proposition 'Socrates is not white'. If anything else be negatively predicated of the subject or if anything else be the subject though the predicate remain the same, the denial will not be the denial proper to that affirmation, but on that is distinct.

The denial proper to the affirmation 'every man is white' is 'not every man is white'; that proper to the affirmation 'some men are white' is 'no man is white', while that proper to the affirmation 'man is white' is 'man is not white'.

We have shown further that a single denial is contradictorily opposite to a single affirmation and we have explained which these are; we have also stated that contrary are distinct from contradictory propositions and which the contrary are; also that with regard to a pair of opposite propositions it is not always the case that one is true and the other false. We have pointed out, moreover, what the reason of this is and under what circumstances the truth of the one involves the falsity of the other.

Part 8

An affirmation or denial is single, if it indicates some one fact about some one subject; it matters not whether the subject is universal and whether the statement has a universal character, or whether this is not so. Such single propositions are: 'every man is white', 'not every man is white';'man is white','man is not white'; 'no man is white', 'some men are white'; provided the word 'white' has one meaning. If, on the other hand, one word has two meanings which do not combine to form one, the affirmation is not single. For instance, if a man should establish the symbol 'garment' as significant both of a horse and of a man, the proposition 'garment is white' would not be a single affirmation, nor its opposite a single denial. For it is equivalent to the proposition 'horse and man are white', which, again, is equivalent to the two propositions 'horse is white', 'man is white'. If, then, these two propositions have more than a single significance, and do not form a single proposition, it is plain that the first proposition either has more than one significance or else has none; for a particular man is not a horse.

This, then, is another instance of those propositions of which both the positive and the negative forms may be true or false simultaneously.

Part 9

In the case of that which is or which has taken place, propositions, whether positive or negative, must be true or false. Again, in the case of a pair of contradictories, either when the subject is universal and the propositions are of a universal character, or when it is individual, as has been said,' one of the two must be true and the other false; whereas when the subject is universal, but the propositions are not of a universal character, there is no such necessity. We have discussed this type also in a previous chapter.

When the subject, however, is individual, and that which is predicated of it relates to the future, the case is altered. For if all propositions whether positive or negative are either true or false, then any given predicate must either belong to the subject or not, so that if one man affirms that an event of a given character will take place and another denies it, it is plain that the statement of the one will correspond with reality and that of the other will not. For the predicate cannot both belong and not belong to the subject at one and the same time with regard to the future.

Thus, if it is true to say that a thing is white, it must necessarily be white; if the reverse proposition is true, it will of necessity not be white. Again, if it is white, the proposition stating that it is white was true; if it is not white, the proposition to the opposite effect was true. And if it is not white, the man who states that it is making a false statement; and if the man who states that it is white is making a false statement, it follows that it is not white. It may therefore be argued that it is necessary that affirmations or denials must be either true or false.

Now if this be so, nothing is or takes place fortuitously, either in the present or in the future, and there are no real alternatives; everything takes place of necessity and is fixed. For either he that affirms that it will take place or he that denies this is in correspondence with fact, whereas if things did not take place of necessity, an event might just as easily not happen as happen; for the meaning of the word 'fortuitous' with regard to present or future events is that reality is so constituted that it may issue in either of two opposite directions. Again, if a thing is white now, it was true before to say that it would be white, so that of anything that has taken place it was always true to say 'it is' or 'it will be'. But if it was always true to say that a thing is or will be, it is not possible that it should not be or not be about to be, and when a thing cannot not come to be, it is impossible that it should not come to be, and when it is impossible that it should not come to be, it must come to be. All, then, that is about to be must of necessity take place. It results from this that nothing is uncertain or fortuitous, for if it were fortuitous it would not be necessary.

Again, to say that neither the affirmation nor the denial is true, maintaining, let us say, that an event neither will take place nor will not take place, is to take up a position impossible to defend. In the first place, though facts should prove the one proposition false, the opposite would still be untrue. Secondly, if it was true to say that a thing was both white and large, both these qualities must necessarily belong to it; and if they will belong to it the next day, they must necessarily belong to it the next day. But if an event is neither to take place nor not to take place the next day, the element of chance will be eliminated. For example, it would be necessary that a sea-fight should neither take place nor fail to take place on the next day.

These awkward results and others of the same kind follow, if it is an irrefragable law that of every pair of contradictory propositions, whether they have regard to universals and are stated as universally applicable, or whether they have regard to individuals, one must be true and the other false, and that there are no real alternatives, but that all that is or takes place is the outcome of necessity. There would be no need to deliberate or to take trouble, on the supposition that if we should adopt a certain course, a certain result would follow, while, if we did not, the result would not follow. For a man may predict an event ten thousand years beforehand, and another may predict the reverse; that which was truly predicted at the moment in the past will of necessity take place in the fullness of time.

Further, it makes no difference whether people have or have not actually made the contradictory statements. For it is manifest that the circumstances are not influenced by the fact of an affirmation or denial on the part of anyone. For events will not take place or fail to take place because it was stated that they would or would not take place, nor is this any more the case if the prediction dates back ten thousand years or any other space of time. Wherefore, if through all time the nature of things was so constituted that a prediction about an event was true, then through all time it was necessary that that should find fulfillment; and with regard to all events, circumstances have always been such that their occurrence is a matter of necessity. For that of which someone has said truly that it will be, cannot fail to take place; and of that which takes place, it was always true to say that it would be.

Yet this view leads to an impossible conclusion; for we see that both deliberation and action are causative with regard to the future, and that, to speak more generally, in those things which are not continuously actual there is potentiality in either direction. Such things may either be or not be; events also therefore may either take place or not take place. There are many obvious instances of this. It is possible that this coat may be cut in half, and yet it may not be cut in half, but wear out first. In the same way, it is possible that it should not be cut in half; unless this were so, it would not be possible that it should wear out first. So it is therefore with all other events which possess this kind of potentiality. It is therefore plain that it is not of necessity that everything is or takes place; but in some instances there are real alternatives, in which case the affirmation is no more true and no more false than the denial; while some exhibit a predisposition

125

and general tendency in one direction or the other, and yet can issue in the opposite direction by exception.

Now that which is must needs be when it is, and that which is not must needs not be when it is not. Yet it cannot be said without qualification that all existence and non-existence is the outcome of necessity. For there is a difference between saying that that which is, when it is, must needs be, and simply saying that all that is must needs be, and similarly in the case of that which is not. In the case, also, of two contradictory propositions this holds good. Everything must either be or not be, whether in the present or in the future, but it is not always possible to distinguish and state determinately which of these alternatives must necessarily come about.

Let me illustrate. A sea-fight must either take place to-morrow or not, but it is not necessary that it should take place to-morrow, neither is it necessary that it should not take place, yet it is necessary that it either should or should not take place to-morrow. Since propositions correspond with facts, it is evident that when in future events there is a real alternative, and a potentiality in contrary directions, the corresponding affirmation and denial have the same character.

This is the case with regard to that which is not always existent or not always nonexistent. One of the two propositions in such instances must be true and the other false, but we cannot say determinately that this or that is false, but must leave the alternative undecided. One may indeed be more likely to be true than the other, but it cannot be either actually true or actually false. It is therefore plain that it is not necessary that of an affirmation and a denial one should be true and the other false. For in the case of that which exists potentially, but not actually, the rule which applies to that which exists actually does not hold good. The case is rather as we have indicated.

Part 10

An affirmation is the statement of a fact with regard to a subject, and this subject is either a noun or that which has no name; the subject and predicate in an affirmation must each denote a single thing. I have already explained' what is meant by a noun and by that which has no name; for I stated that the expression 'not-man' was not a noun, in the proper sense of the word, but an indefinite noun, denoting as it does in a certain sense a single thing. Similarly the expression 'does not enjoy health' is not a verb proper, but an indefinite verb. Every affirmation, then, and every denial, will consist of a noun and a verb, either definite or indefinite.

There can be no affirmation or denial without a verb; for the expressions 'is', 'will be', 'was', 'is coming to be', and the like are verbs according to our definition, since besides their specific meaning they convey the notion of time. Thus the primary affirmation and denial are 'as follows: 'man is', 'man is not'. Next to these, there are the propositions: 'not-man is', 'not-man is not'. Again we have the propositions: 'every man is, 'every man is not', 'all that is not-man is', 'all that is not-man is not'. The same classification holds good with regard to such periods of time as lie outside the present.

When the verb 'is' is used as a third element in the sentence, there can be positive and negative propositions of two sorts. Thus in the sentence 'man is just' the verb 'is' is used as a third element, call it verb or noun, which you will. Four propositions, therefore, instead of two can be formed with these materials. Two of the four, as regards their affirmation and denial, correspond in their logical sequence with the propositions which deal with a condition of privation; the other two do not correspond with these.

I mean that the verb 'is' is added either to the term 'just' or to the term 'not-just', and two negative propositions are formed in the same way. Thus we have the four propositions. Reference to the subjoined table will make matters clear:

A. Affirmation B. Denial Man is just Man is not just \ / X / \ D. Denial C. Affirmation Man is not not-just Man is not-just Here 'is' and 'is not' are added either to 'just' or to 'not-just'. This then is the proper scheme for these propositions, as has been said in the Analytics. The same rule holds good, if the subject is distributed. Thus we have the table:

A'. Affirmation B'. Denial Every man is just Not every man is just \ / X D'. Denial / \ C'. Affirmation
Not every man is not-just Every man is not-just Yet here it is not possible, in the same way as in the former case, that the propositions joined in the table by a diagonal line should both be true; though under certain circumstances this is the case.

We have thus set out two pairs of opposite propositions; there are moreover two other pairs, if a term be conjoined with 'not-man', the latter forming a kind of subject. Thus:

A." B." Not-man is just Not-man is not just \ / - X

D." / \ C." Not-man is not not-just Not-man is not-just

This is an exhaustive enumeration of all the pairs of opposite propositions that can possibly be framed. This last group should remain distinct from those which preceded it, since it employs as its subject the expression 'not-man'.

When the verb 'is' does not fit the structure of the sentence (for instance, when the verbs 'walks', 'enjoys health' are used), that scheme applies, which applied when the word 'is' was added.

Thus we have the propositions: 'every man enjoys health', 'every man does-not-enjoy-health', 'all that is not-man enjoys health', 'all that is not-man does-not-enjoy-health'. We must not in these propositions use the expression 'not every man'. The negative must be attached to the word 'man', for the word 'every' does not give to the subject a universal significance, but implies that, as a subject, it is distributed. This is plain from the following pairs: 'man enjoys health', 'man does not enjoy health'; 'not-man enjoys health', 'not man does not enjoy health'. These propositions differ from the former in being indefinite and not universal in character. Thus the adjectives 'every' and no additional significance except that the subject, whether in a positive or in a negative sentence, is distributed. The rest of the sentence, therefore, will in each case be the same.

Since the contrary of the proposition 'every animal is just' is 'no animal is just', it is plain that these two propositions will never both be true at the same time or with reference to the

129

same subject. Sometimes, however, the contradictories of these contraries will both be true, as in the instance before us: the propositions 'not every animal is just' and 'some animals are just' are both true.

Further, the proposition 'no man is just' follows from the proposition 'every man is not just' and the proposition 'not every man is not just', which is the opposite of 'every man is not-just', follows from the proposition 'some men are just'; for if this be true, there must be some just men.

It is evident, also, that when the subject is individual, if a question is asked and the negative answer is the true one, a certain positive proposition is also true. Thus, if the question were asked Socrates wise?' and the negative answer were the true one, the positive inference 'Then Socrates is unwise' is correct. But no such inference is correct in the case of universals, but rather a negative proposition. For instance, if to the question 'Is every man wise?' the answer is 'no', the inference 'Then every man is unwise' is false. But under these circumstances the inference 'Not every man is wise' is correct. This last is the contradictory, the former the contrary. Negative expressions, which consist of an indefinite noun or predicate, such as 'not-man' or 'not-just', may seem to be denials containing neither noun nor verb in the proper sense of the words. But they are not. For a denial must always be either true or false, and he that uses the expression 'not man', if nothing more be added, is not nearer but rather further from making a true or a false statement than he who uses the expression 'man'.

The propositions 'everything that is not man is just', and the contradictory of this, are not equivalent to any of the other propositions; on the other hand, the proposition 'everything that is not man is not just' is equivalent to the proposition 'nothing that is not man is just'.

The conversion of the position of subject and predicate in a sentence involves no difference in its meaning. Thus we say 'man is white' and 'white is man'. If these were not equivalent, there would be more than one contradictory to the same proposition, whereas it has been demonstrated' that each proposition has one proper contradictory and one only. For of the proposition 'man is white' the appropriate contradictory is 'man is not white', and of the proposition 'white is man', if its meaning be different, the contradictory will either be 'white is not not-man' or 'white is not man'. Now the former of these is the contradictory of the proposition 'white is not-man', and the latter of these is the contradictory of the proposition 'man is white'; thus there will be two contradictories to one proposition.

It is evident, therefore, that the inversion of the relative position of subject and predicate does not affect the sense of affirmations and denials.

Section 2

Part 11

There is no unity about an affirmation or denial which, either positively or negatively, predicates one thing of many subjects, or many things of the same subject, unless that which is indicated by the many is really some one thing. do not apply this word 'one' to those things which, though they have a single recognized name, yet do not combine to form a unity. Thus, man may be an animal, and biped, and domesticated, but these three predicates combine to form a unity. On the other hand, the predicates 'white', 'man', and 'walking' do not thus combine. Neither, therefore, if these three form the subject of an affirmation, nor if they form its predicate, is there any unity about that affirmation. In both cases the unity is linguistic, but not real.

If therefore the dialectical question is a request for an answer, i.e. either for the admission of a premiss or for the admission of one of two contradictories-and the premiss is itself always one of two contradictories-the answer to such a question as contains the above predicates cannot be a single proposition. For as I have explained in the Topics, question is not a single one, even if the answer asked for is true.

At the same time it is plain that a question of the form 'what is it?' is not a dialectical question, for a dialectical questioner must by the form of his question give his opponent the chance of announcing one of two alternatives, whichever he wishes. He must therefore put the question into a more definite form, and inquire, e.g.. whether man has such and such a characteristic or not.

Some combinations of predicates are such that the separate predicates unite to form a single predicate. Let us consider under what conditions this is and is not possible. We may either state in two separate propositions that man is an animal and that man is a biped, or we may combine the two, and state that man is an animal with two feet. Similarly we may use 'man' and 'white' as separate predicates, or unite them into one. Yet if a man is a shoemaker and is also good, we cannot construct a composite proposition and say that he is a good shoemaker. For if, whenever two separate predicates truly belong to a subject, it follows that the predicate resulting from their combination also truly belongs to the subject, many absurd results ensue. For instance, a man is man and white. Therefore, if predicates may always be combined, he is a white man. Again, if the predicate 'white' belongs to him, then the combination of that predicate with the former composite predicate will be permissible. Thus it will be right to say that he is a white man so on indefinitely. Or, again, we may combine the predicates 'musical', 'white', and 'walking', and these may be combined many times. Similarly we may say that Socrates is Socrates and a man, and that therefore he is the man Socrates, or that Socrates is a man and a biped, and that therefore he is a two-footed man. Thus it is manifest that if man states unconditionally that predicates can always be combined, many absurd consequences ensue.

We will now explain what ought to be laid down.
Those predicates, and terms forming the subject of predication, which are accidental either to the same subject or to one another, do not combine to form a unity. Take the proposition 'man is white of complexion and musical'. Whiteness and being musical do not coalesce to form a unity, for they belong only accidentally to the same subject. Nor yet, if it were true to say that that which is white is musical, would the terms 'musical' and 'white' form a unity, for it is only incidentally that that which is musical is white; the combination of the two will, therefore, not form a unity.

Thus, again, whereas, if a man is both good and a shoemaker, we cannot combine the two propositions and say simply that he is a good shoemaker, we are, at the same time, able to combine the predicates 'animal' and 'biped' and say that a man is an animal with two feet, for these predicates are not accidental.

Those predicates, again, cannot form a unity, of which the one is implicit in the other: thus we cannot combine the predicate 'white' again and again with that which already contains the notion 'white', nor is it right to call a man an animal-man or a two-footed man; for the notions 'animal' and 'biped' are implicit in the word 'man'. On the other hand, it is possible to predicate a term simply of any one instance, and to say that some one particular man is a man or that some one white man is a white man.

Yet this is not always possible: indeed, when in the adjunct there is some opposite which involves a contradiction, the predication of the simple term is impossible. Thus it is not right to call a dead man a man. When, however, this is not the case, it is not impossible.

Yet the facts of the case might rather be stated thus: when some such opposite elements are present, resolution is never possible, but when they are not present, resolution is nevertheless not always possible. Take the proposition 'Homer is so-and-so', say 'a poet'; does it follow that Homer is, or does it not? The verb 'is' is here used of Homer only incidentally, the proposition being that Homer is a poet, not that he is, in the independent sense of the word.

Thus, in the case of those predications which have within them no contradiction when the nouns are expanded into definitions, and wherein the predicates belong to the subject in their own proper sense and not in any indirect way, the individual may be the subject of the simple propositions as well as of the composite. But in the case of that which is not, it is not true to say that because it is the object of opinion, it is; for the opinion held about it is that it is not, not that it is.

Part 12

As these distinctions have been made, we must consider the mutual relation of those affirmations and denials which assert or deny possibility or contingency, impossibility or necessity: for the subject is not without difficulty.

We admit that of composite expressions those are contradictory each to each which have the verb 'to be' its positive and negative form respectively. Thus the contradictory of the proposition 'man is' is 'man is not', not 'not-man is', and the contradictory of 'man is white' is 'man is not white', not 'man is not-white'. For otherwise, since either the positive or the negative proposition is true of any subject, it will turn out true to say that a piece of wood is a man that is not white.

Now if this is the case, in those propositions which do not contain the verb 'to be' the verb which takes its place will exercise the same function. Thus the contradictory of 'man walks' is 'man does not walk', not 'not-man walks'; for to say 'man walks' merely equivalent to saying 'man is walking'.

If then this rule is universal, the contradictory of 'it may be' is may not be', not 'it cannot be'.

Now it appears that the same thing both may and may not be; for instance, everything that may be cut or may walk may also escape cutting and refrain from walking; and the reason is that those things that have potentiality in this sense are not always actual. In such cases, both the positive and the negative propositions will be true; for that which is capable of walking or of being seen has also a potentiality in the opposite direction.

But since it is impossible that contradictory propositions should both be true of the same subject, it follows that' it may not be' is not the contradictory of 'it may be'. For it is a logical consequence of what we have said, either that the same predicate can be both applicable and inapplicable to one and the same subject at the same time, or that it is not by the addition of the verbs 'be' and 'not be', respectively, that positive and negative propositions are formed. If the former of these alternatives must be rejected, we must choose the latter.

The contradictory, then, of 'it may be' is 'it cannot be'. The same rule applies to the proposition 'it is contingent that it should be'; the contradictory of this is 'it is not contingent that it should be'. The similar propositions, such as 'it is necessary' and 'it is impossible', may be dealt with in the same manner. For it comes about that just as in the former instances the verbs 'is' and 'is not' were added to the subject-matter of the sentence 'white' and 'man', so here 'that it should be' and 'that it should not be' are the subject-matter and 'is possible', 'is contingent', are added. These indicate that a certain thing is or is not possible, just as in the former instances 'is' and 'is not' indicated that certain things were or were not the case.

The contradictory, then, of 'it may not be' is not 'it cannot be', but 'it cannot not be', and the contradictory of 'it may be' is not 'it may not be', but cannot be'. Thus the propositions 'it may be' and 'it may not be' appear each to imply the other: for, since these two propositions are not contradictory, the same thing both may and may not be. But the propositions 'it may be' and 'it cannot be' can never be true of the same subject at the same time, for they are contradictory. Nor can the propositions 'it may not be' and 'it cannot not be' be at once true of the same subject.

The propositions which have to do with necessity are governed by the same principle. The contradictory of 'it is necessary that it should be', is not 'it is necessary that it should not be,' but 'it is not necessary that it should be', and the contradictory of 'it is necessary that it should not be' is 'it is not necessary that it should not be'.

Again, the contradictory of 'it is impossible that it should be' is not 'it is impossible that it should not be' but 'it is not impossible that it should be', and the contradictory of 'it is impossible that it should not be' is 'it is not impossible that it should not be'.

To generalize, we must, as has been stated, define the clauses 'that it should be' and 'that it should not be' as the subject-matter of the propositions, and in making these terms into affirmations and denials we must combine them with 'that it should be' and 'that it should not be' respectively.

We must consider the following pairs as contradictory propositions:

It may be. It cannot be.
It is contingent. It is not contingent.
It is impossible. It is not impossible.
It is necessary. It is not necessary.
It is true. It is not true.

Part 13

Logical sequences follow in due course when we have arranged the propositions thus. From the proposition 'it may be' it follows that it is contingent, and the relation is reciprocal. It follows also that it is not impossible and not necessary.

From the proposition 'it may not be' or 'it is contingent that it should not be' it follows that it is not necessary that it should not be and that it is not impossible that it should not be. From the proposition 'it cannot be' or 'it is not contingent' it follows that it is necessary that it should not be and that it is impossible that it should be. From the proposition 'it cannot not be' or 'it is not contingent that it should not be' it follows that it is necessary that it should be and that it is impossible that it should not be.

Let us consider these statements by the help of a table:

A. B.
It may be. It cannot be.
It is contingent. It is not contingent.
It is not impossible It is impossible that it

that it should be. should be.
It is not necessary It is necessary that it

that it should be. should not be.

C. D.
It may not be. It cannot not be.
It is contingent that it It is not contingent that

should not be. it should not be.
It is not impossible It is impossible thatit

that it should not be. should not be.
It is not necessary that It is necessary that it

it should not be. should be.

Now the propositions 'it is impossible that it should be' and 'it is not impossible that it should be' are consequent upon the propositions 'it may be', 'it is contingent', and 'it cannot be', 'it is not contingent', the contradictories upon the contradictories. But there is inversion. The negative of the proposition 'it is impossible' is consequent upon the proposition 'it may be' and the corresponding positive in the first case upon the negative in the second. For 'it is impossible' is a positive proposition and 'it is not impossible' is negative.

We must investigate the relation subsisting between these propositions and those which predicate necessity. That there is a distinction is clear. In this case, contrary propositions follow respectively from contradictory propositions, and the contradictory propositions belong to separate sequences. For the proposition 'it is not necessary that it should be' is not the negative of 'it is necessary that it should not be', for both these propositions may be true of the same subject; for when it is necessary that a thing should not be, it is not necessary that it should be. The reason why the propositions predicating necessity do not follow in the same kind of sequence as the rest, lies in the fact that the proposition 'it is impossible' is equivalent, when used with a contrary subject, to the proposition 'it is necessary'. For when it is impossible that a thing should be, it is necessary, not that it should be, but that it should not be, and when it is impossible that a thing should not be, it is necessary that it should be. Thus, if the propositions predicating impossibility or non-impossibility follow without change of subject from those predicating possibility or non-possibility, those predicating necessity must follow with the contrary subject; for the propositions 'it is impossible' and 'it is necessary' are not equivalent, but, as has been said, inversely connected.

Yet perhaps it is impossible that the contradictory propositions predicating necessity should be thus arranged. For when it is necessary that a thing should be, it is possible that it should be. (For if not, the opposite follows, since one or the other must follow; so, if it is not possible, it is impossible, and it is thus impossible that a thing should be, which must necessarily be; which is absurd.)

Yet from the proposition 'it may be' it follows that it is not impossible, and from that it follows that it is not necessary; it comes about therefore that the thing which must necessarily be need not be; which is absurd. But again, the proposition 'it is necessary that it should be' does not follow from the proposition 'it may be', nor does the proposition 'it is necessary that it should not be'. For the proposition 'it may be' implies a twofold possibility, while, if either of the two former propositions is true, the twofold possibility vanishes.

For if a thing may be, it may also not be, but if it is necessary that it should be or that it should not be, one of the two alternatives will be excluded. It remains, therefore, that the proposition 'it is not necessary that it should not be' follows from the proposition 'it may be'. For this is true also of that which must necessarily be.

Moreover the proposition 'it is not necessary that it should not be' is the contradictory of that which follows from the proposition 'it cannot be'; for 'it cannot be' is followed by 'it is impossible that it should be' and by 'it is necessary that it should not be', and the contradictory of this is the proposition 'it is not necessary that it should not be'. Thus in this case also contradictory propositions follow contradictory in the way indicated, and no logical impossibilities occur when they are thus arranged.

It may be questioned whether the proposition 'it may be' follows from the proposition 'it is necessary that it should be'. If not, the contradictory must follow, namely that it cannot be, or, if a man should maintain that this is not the contradictory, then the proposition 'it may not be'.

Now both of these are false of that which necessarily is. At the same time, it is thought that if a thing may be cut it may also not be cut, if a thing may be it may also not be, and thus it would follow that a thing which must necessarily be may possibly not be; which is false. It is evident, then, that it is not always the case that that which may be or may walk possesses also a potentiality in the other direction. There are exceptions. In the first place we must except those things which possess a potentiality not in accordance with a rational principle, as fire possesses the potentiality of giving out heat, that is, an irrational capacity. Those potentialities which involve a rational principle are potentialities of more than one result, that is, of contrary results; those that are irrational are not always thus constituted. As I have said, fire cannot both heat and not heat, neither has anything that is always actual any twofold potentiality. Yet some even of those potentialities which are irrational admit of opposite results. However, thus much has been said to emphasize the truth that it is not every potentiality which admits of opposite results, even where the word is used always in the same sense.

But in some cases the word is used equivocally. For the term 'possible' is ambiguous, being used in the one case with reference to facts, to that which is actualized, as when a man is said to find walking possible because he is actually walking, and generally when a capacity is predicated because it is actually realized; in the other case, with reference to a state in which realization is conditionally practicable, as when a man is said to find walking possible because under certain conditions he would walk. This last sort of potentiality belongs only to that which can be in motion, the former can exist also in the case of that which has not this power. Both of that which is walking and is actual, and of that which has the capacity though not necessarily realized, it is true to say that it is not impossible that it should walk (or, in the other case, that it should be), but while we cannot predicate this latter kind of potentiality of that which is necessary in the unqualified sense of the word, we can predicate the former.

Our conclusion, then, is this: that since the universal is consequent upon the particular, that which is necessary is also possible, though not in every sense in which the word may be used.

We may perhaps state that necessity and its absence are the initial principles of existence and non-existence, and that all else must be regarded as posterior to these.

It is plain from what has been said that that which is of necessity is actual. Thus, if that which is eternal is prior, actuality also is prior to potentiality. Some things are actualities without potentiality, namely, the primary substances; a second class consists of those things which are actual but also potential, whose actuality is in nature prior to their potentiality, though posterior in time; a third class comprises those things which are never actualized, but are pure potentialities.

Part 14

The question arises whether an affirmation finds its contrary in a denial or in another affirmation; whether the proposition 'every man is just' finds its contrary in the proposition 'no man is just', or in the proposition 'every man is unjust'. Take the propositions 'Callias is just', 'Callias is not just', 'Callias is unjust'; we have to discover which of these form contraries.

Now if the spoken word corresponds with the judgement of the mind, and if, in thought, that judgement is the contrary of another, which pronounces a contrary fact, in the way, for instance, in which the judgement 'every man is just' pronounces a contrary to that pronounced by the judgement 'every man is unjust', the same must needs hold good with regard to spoken affirmations.

But if, in thought, it is not the judgement which pronounces a contrary fact that is the contrary of another, then one affirmation will not find its contrary in another, but rather in the corresponding denial. We must therefore consider which true judgement is the contrary of the false, that which forms the denial of the false judgement or that which affirms the contrary fact.

Let me illustrate. There is a true judgement concerning that which is good, that it is good; another, a false judgement, that it is not good; and a third, which is distinct, that it is bad. Which of these two is contrary to the true? And if they are one and the same, which mode of expression forms the contrary?

It is an error to suppose that judgements are to be defined as contrary in virtue of the fact that they have contrary subjects; for the judgement concerning a good thing, that it is good, and that concerning a bad thing, that it is bad, may be one and the same, and whether they are so or not, they both represent the truth. Yet the subjects here are contrary. But judgements are not contrary because they have contrary subjects, but because they are to the contrary effect.

Now if we take the judgement that that which is good is good, and another that it is not good, and if there are at the same time other attributes, which do not and cannot belong to the good, we must nevertheless refuse to treat as the contraries of the true judgement those which opine that some other attribute subsists which does not subsist, as also those that opine that some other attribute does not subsist which does subsist, for both these classes of judgement are of unlimited content.

Those judgements must rather be termed contrary to the true judgements, in which error is present. Now these judgements are those which are concerned with the starting points of generation, and generation is the passing from one extreme to its opposite; therefore error is a like transition.

Now that which is good is both good and not bad. The first quality is part of its essence, the second accidental; for it is by accident that it is not bad. But if that true judgement is most really true, which concerns the subject's intrinsic nature, then that false judgement likewise is most really false, which concerns its intrinsic nature. Now the judgement that that is good is not good is a false judgement concerning its intrinsic nature, the judgement that it is bad is one concerning that which is accidental. Thus the judgement which denies the true judgement is more really false than that which positively asserts the presence of the contrary quality. But it is the man who forms that judgement which is contrary to the true who is most thoroughly deceived, for contraries are among the things which differ most widely within the same class. If then of the two judgements one is contrary to the true judgement, but that which is contradictory is the more truly contrary, then the latter, it seems, is the real contrary. The judgement that that which is good is bad is composite. For presumably the man who forms that judgement must at the same time understand that that which is good is not good.

Further, the contradictory is either always the contrary or never; therefore, if it must necessarily be so in all other cases, our conclusion in the case just dealt with would seem to be correct. Now where terms have no contrary, that judgement is false, which forms the negative of the true; for instance, he who thinks a man is not a man forms a false judgement. If then in these cases the negative is the contrary, then the principle is universal in its application.

Again, the judgement that that which is not good is not good is parallel with the judgement that that which is good is good. Besides these there is the judgement that that which is good is not good, parallel with the judgement that that that is not good is good. Let us consider, therefore, what would form the contrary of the true judgement that that which is not good is not good. The judgement that it is bad would, of course, fail to meet the case, since two true judgements are never contrary and this judgement might be true at the same time as that with which it is connected. For since some things which are not good are bad, both judgements may be true. Nor is the judgement that it is not bad the contrary, for this too might be true, since both qualities might be predicated of the same subject. It remains, therefore, that of the judgement concerning that which is not good, that it is not good, the contrary judgement is that it is good; for this is false. In the same way, moreover, the judgement concerning that which is good, that it is not good, is the contrary of the judgement that it is good.

It is evident that it will make no difference if we universalize the positive judgement, for the universal negative judgement will form the contrary. For instance, the contrary of the judgement that everything that is good is good is that nothing that is good is good. For the judgement that that which is good is good, if the subject be understood in a universal sense, is equivalent to the judgement that whatever is good is good, and this is identical with the judgement that everything that is good is good. We may deal similarly with judgements concerning that which is not good.

If therefore this is the rule with judgements, and if spoken affirmations and denials are judgements expressed in words, it is plain that the universal denial is the contrary of the affirmation about the same subject. Thus the propositions 'everything good is good', 'every man is good', have for their contraries the propositions 'nothing good is good', 'no man is good'. The contradictory propositions, on the other hand, are 'not everything good is good', 'not every man is good'.

It is evident, also, that neither true judgements nor true propositions can be contrary the one to the other. For whereas, when two propositions are true, a man may state both at the same time without inconsistency, contrary propositions are those which state contrary conditions, and contrary conditions cannot subsist at one and the same time in the same subject.

From Aristotle, *Topics* I.7:

First of all we must define the number of senses borne by the term 'Sameness'. Sameness would be generally regarded as falling, roughly speaking, into three divisions. We generally apply the term numerically or specifically or generically-numerically in cases where there is more than one name but only one thing, e.g. 'doublet' and 'cloak';

specifically, where there is more than one thing, but they present no differences in respect of their species, as one man and another, or one horse and another: for things like this that fall under the same species are said to be 'specifically the same'. Similarly, too, those things are called generically the same which fall under the same genus, such as a horse and a man. It might appear that the sense in which water from the same spring is called 'the same water' is somehow different and unlike the senses mentioned above: but really such a case as this ought to be ranked in the same class with the things that in one way or another are called 'the same' in view of unity of species. For all such things seem to be of one family and to resemble one another. For the reaon why all water is said to be specifically the same as all other water is because of a certain likeness it bears to it, and the only difference in the case of water drawn from the same spring is this, that the likeness is more emphatic: that is why we do not distinguish it from the things that in one way or another are called 'the same' in view of unity of species. It is generally supposed that the term 'the same' is most used in a sense agreed on by every one when applied to what is numerically one. But even so, it is apt to be rendered in more than one sense; its most literal and primary use is found whenever the sameness is rendered in reference to an alternative name or definition, as when a cloak is said to be the same as a doublet, or an animal that walks on two feet is said to be the same as a man: a second sense is when it is rendered in reference to a property, as when what can acquire knowledge is called the same as a man, and what naturally travels upward the same as fire: while a third use is found when it is rendered in reference to some term drawn from Accident, as when the creature who is sitting, or who is musical, is called the same as Socrates. For all these

148

uses mean to signify numerical unity. That what I have just said is true may be best seen where one form of appellation is substituted for another. For often when we give the order to call one of the people who are sitting down, indicating him by name, we change our description, whenever the person to whom we give the order happens not to understand us; he will, we think, understand better from some accidental feature; so we bid him call to us 'the man who is sitting' or 'who is conversing over there'-clearly supposing ourselves to be indicating the same object by its name and by its accident.

From St. Thomas Aquinas, *Commentary on On Interpretation* III.4:

The conceptions of the intellect are likenesses of things and therefore the things that are in the intellect can be considered and named in two ways: according to themselves, and according to the nature of the things of which they are likenesses. For just as a statue – say of Hercules – in itself is called and is "bronze" but as it is a likeness of Hercules is named "man," so if we consider the things that are in the intellect in themselves, there is always composition where there is truth and falsity, for they are never found in the intellect as it compares one simple concept with another. But if the composition is referred to a reality, it is sometimes called composition, sometimes division: composition when the intellect compares one concept to another as though apprehending a conjunction or identity of the things of which they are the conceptions; division, when it so compares one concept with another that it apprehends the things to be diverse. In vocal sound, therefore, affirmation is called composition inasmuch as it signifies a conjunction on the part of the thing and negation is called division inasmuch as it signifies the separation of things.

From St. Thomas Aquinas, *Commentary on On Interpretation* **III.9:**

To know this relationship of conformity is to judge that a thing is such or is not, which is to compose and divide; therefore, the intellect does not know truth except by composing and dividing through its judgment. If the judgment is in accordance with things it will be true, i.e., when the intellect judges a thing to be what it is or not to be what it is not. The judgment will be false when it is not in accordance with the thing, i.e., when it judges that what is, is not, or that what is not, is. It is evident from this that truth and falsity as it is in the one knowing and speaking is had only in composition and division.

From St. Thomas Aquinas, *Commentary on On Interpretation* **X.14, 16:**

There are, therefore, three kinds of affirmations in which something is predicated of a universal: in one, something is predicated of the universal universally, as in "every man is an animal;" in another, something is predicated of the universal particularly, as in "some man is white." The third affirmation is that in which something is predicated of the universal without a determination of universality or particularity. Enunciation of this kind is customarily called indefinite...If we add the singular to the three already mentioned there will be four modes of enunciation pertaining to quantity: universal, singular, indefinite, and particular.

JUDGMENT - COMMENTARY

Subject - what you are talking about.
Predicate - what you are saying about it.

God	is	love.		Love	is	God.
|		|	vs.	|		|
Subject		*Predicate*		*Subject*		*Predicate*

Kinds of Propositions:
- **Categorical Proposition:** Men are pigs.
- **Compound Propositions:**
   - **Hypothetical:** If men eat ham, then men are pigs.
   - **Disjunctive:** Either men are dogs or men are pigs.
   - **Conjunctive:** Men are both dogs and pigs.

Quantity of Propositions:
- **Universal** = "All men are pigs"
   (**Singulars** are treated as universals: "Jimmy is a pig")
- **Particular** = "Some men are pigs"
   (includes "most," "many," etc.)

Quality of Propositions:
- **Affirmative** = "All men are pigs"
- **Negative** = "No men are pigs"

Four types of Propositions:
A - Universal Affirmative (All S is P)
E - Universal Negative (No S is P)
I - Particular Affirmative (Some S is P)
O - Particular Negative (Some S is not P)

Memorize

151

Distribution:

A term is **distributed** when it refers to *all*;
      undistributed when it refers to *some*.

- The **Subject** of a <u>Universal</u> Proposition (A or E)
      is always distributed.
- The **Predicate** of a <u>Negative</u> Proposition (E or O)
      is always distributed.

          A - All S^d is P^u
          E - No S^d is P^d
          I - Some S^u is P^u
          O - Some S^u is not P^d

Changing Propositions:
- **Conversion** - Switch Subject and Predicate. Valid with E
   and I Propositions:
       E - No men are pigs → No pigs are men
       I - Some men are pigs → Some pigs are men

- **Obversion** - Negate the Copula and the Predicate. Valid
   with all Propositions:
       A - All men are pigs → No men are non-pigs (E)
       E - No men are pigs → All men are non-pigs (A)
       I - Some men are pigs → Some men are not non-pigs (O)
       O - Some men are not pigs → Some men are non-pigs (I)
* Note that the Proposition changes type, and that I and O
   obversions are basically worthless.

Types of Opposition:

(**Opposition:** a relation between two Propositions that have the same Subject and Predicate.)

- **Contradiction** - if one is true, the other is false, if one is false, the other is true.
- **Contrariety** - cannot both be true, but can both be false.
- **Subcontrariety** - can both be true but cannot both be false.
- **Subalternation** - if the universal is true, then the particular is true.
- **Superalternation** - if the particular is false, then the universal is false.

The Square of Opposition:

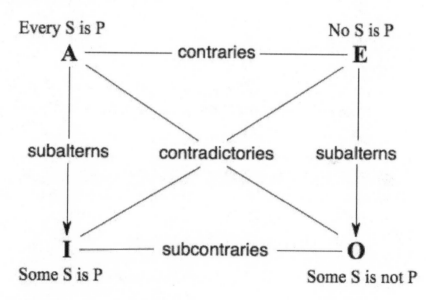

JUDGMENT – SUPPLEMENT
From Catch-22 by Joseph Heller

*Private Clevinger is being accused in a private military court of making a statement about their ability to punish him. **The Colonel** and **Major Metcalf** are examining the witness, and **Lieutenant Scheisskopf** is both prosecuting and defending attorney.*

Colonel: What did you mean when you said we couldn't punish you?

Clevinger: When, sir?

Colonel: I'm asking the questions. You're answering them.

Clevinger: Yes, sir. I –

Colonel: Did you think we brought you here to ask questions and for me to answer them?

Clevinger: No, sir. I –

Colonel: What did we bring you here for?

Clevinger: To answer questions.

Colonel: You're damned right. Now suppose you start answering some before I break your damned head. Just what the hell did you mean, you bastard, when you said we couldn't punish you?

Clevinger: I don't think I ever made that statement sir.

Colonel: Will you speak up, please? I couldn't hear you.

Clevinger: Yes, sir. I –

Metcalf: Will you speak up, please? He couldn't hear you.

Clevinger: Yes, sir. I –

Colonel: Metcalf.

Metcalf: Sir?

Colonel: Didn't I tell you to keep your stupid mouth shut?

Metcalf: Yes, sir.

Colonel: Then keep your stupid mouth shut when I tell you to keep your stupid mouth shut. Do you understand? Will you speak up, please? I couldn't hear you.

Clevinger: Yes, sir. I –

Colonel: Metcalf, is that your foot I'm stepping on?

Metcalf: No, sir. It must be Lieutenant Scheisskopf's foot.

Scheisskopf: It isn't my foot.

Metcalf: Then maybe it is my foot after all.

Colonel: Move it.

Metcalf: Yes, sir. You'll have to move your foot first, Colonel. It's on top of mine.

Colonel: Are you telling me to move my foot?

Metcalf: No, sir. Oh, no, sir.

Colonel: Then move your foot and keep your stupid mouth shut. Will you speak up, please? I still couldn't hear you.

Clevinger: Yes, sir. I said that I didn't say that you couldn't punish me.

Colonel: Just what the hell are you talking about?

Clevinger: I'm answering your question, sir.

Colonel: What question?

Scheisskopf (*from his notes*): "Just what the hell did you mean, you bastard, when you said we couldn't punish you?"

Colonel: All right. Just what the hell did you mean?

Clevinger: I didn't say you couldn't punish me, sir.

Colonel: When?

Clevinger: When what, sir?

Colonel: Now you're asking me questions again.

Clevinger: I'm sorry, sir. I'm afraid I don't understand your question.

Colonel: When didn't you say we couldn't punish you? Don't you understand my question?

Clevinger: No, sir. I don't understand.

Colonel: You've just told us that. Now suppose you answer my question.

Clevinger: But how can I answer it?

Colonel: That's another question you're asking me.

Clevinger: I'm sorry, sir. But I don't know how to answer it. I never said you couldn't punish me.

Colonel: Now you're telling us when you did say it. I'm asking you to tell us when you didn't say it.

Clevinger (*takes a deep breath*): I always didn't say you couldn't punish me, sir.

REASONING - TEXTS

Aristotle, *Prior Analytics*, tr. A. J. Jenkinson, Selections.

We must first state the subject of our inquiry and the faculty to which it belongs: its subject is demonstration and the faculty that carries it out demonstrative science. We must next define a premiss, a term, and a syllogism, and the nature of a perfect and of an imperfect syllogism; and after that, the inclusion or noninclusion of one term in another as in a whole, and what we mean by predicating one term of all, or none, of another.

A premiss then is a sentence affirming or denying one thing of another. This is either universal or particular or indefinite. By universal I mean the statement that something belongs to all or none of something else; by particular that it belongs to some or not to some or not to all; by indefinite that it does or does not belong, without any mark to show whether it is universal or particular, e.g. 'contraries are subjects of the same science', or 'pleasure is not good'. The demonstrative premiss differs from the dialectical, because the demonstrative premiss is the assertion of one of two contradictory statements (the demonstrator does not ask for his premiss, but lays it down), whereas the dialectical premiss depends on the adversary's choice between two contradictories. But this will make no difference to the production of a syllogism in either case; for both the demonstrator and the dialectician argue syllogistically after stating that something does or does not belong to something else. Therefore a syllogistic premiss without qualification will be an affirmation or denial of something concerning something else in the way we have described; it will be demonstrative, if it is true and obtained through the first principles of its science; while a dialectical premiss is the giving of a choice between two contradictories, when a man is proceeding by question, but when he is syllogizing it is the assertion of that which is apparent and generally admitted, as has been said in the Topics. The nature then of a premiss and the difference between syllogistic, demonstrative, and dialectical premisses, may be taken as sufficiently defined by us in relation to our present need, but will be stated accurately in the sequel.

I call that a term into which the premiss is resolved, i.e. both the predicate and that of which it is predicated, 'being' being added and 'not being' removed, or vice versa.

A syllogism is discourse in which, certain things being stated, something other than what is stated follows of necessity from their being so. I mean by the last phrase that they produce the consequence, and by this, that no further term is required from without in order to make the consequence necessary.

I call that a perfect syllogism which needs nothing other than what has been stated to make plain what necessarily follows; a syllogism is imperfect, if it needs either one or more propositions, which are indeed the necessary consequences of the terms set down, but have not been expressly stated as premisses.

That one term should be included in another as in a whole is the same as for the other to be predicated of all of the first. And we say that one term is predicated of all of another, whenever no instance of the subject can be found of which the other term cannot be asserted: 'to be predicated of none' must be understood in the same way.

4

After these distinctions we now state by what means, when, and how every syllogism is produced; subsequently we must speak of demonstration. Syllogism should be discussed before demonstration because syllogism is the general: the demonstration is a sort of syllogism, but not every syllogism is a demonstration.

Whenever three terms are so related to one another that the last is contained in the middle as in a whole, and the middle is either contained in, or excluded from, the first as in or from a whole, the extremes must be related by a perfect syllogism. I call that term middle which is itself contained in another and contains another in itself: in position also this comes in the middle. By extremes I mean both that term which is itself contained in another and that in which another is contained. If A is predicated of all B, and B of all C, A must be predicated of all C: we have already explained what we mean by 'predicated of all'. Similarly also, if A is predicated of no B, and B of all C, it is necessary that no C will be A.

But if the first term belongs to all the middle, but the middle to none of the last term, there will be no syllogism in respect of the extremes; for nothing necessary follows from the terms being so related; for it is possible that the first should belong either to all or to none of the last, so that neither a particular nor a universal conclusion is necessary. But if there is no necessary consequence, there cannot be a syllogism by means of these premisses. As an example of a universal affirmative relation between the extremes we may take the terms animal, man, horse; of a universal negative relation, the terms animal, man, stone. Nor again can syllogism be formed when neither the first term belongs to any of the middle, nor the middle to any of the last. As an example of a positive relation between the extremes take the terms science, line, medicine: of a negative relation science, line, unit.

If then the terms are universally related, it is clear in this figure when a syllogism will be possible and when not, and that if a syllogism is possible the terms must be related as described, and if they are so related there will be a syllogism. But if one term is related universally, the other in part only, to its subject, there must be a perfect syllogism whenever universality is posited with reference to the major term either affirmatively or negatively, and particularity with reference to the minor term affirmatively: but whenever the universality is posited in relation to the minor term, or the terms are related in any other way, a syllogism is impossible. I call that term the major in which the middle is contained and that term the minor which comes under the middle. Let all B be A and some C be B. Then if 'predicated of all' means what was said above, it is necessary that some C is A. And if no B is A but some C is B, it is necessary that some C is not A. The meaning of 'predicated of none' has also been defined. So there will be a perfect syllogism. This holds good also if the premiss BC should be indefinite, provided that it is affirmative: for we shall have the same syllogism whether the premiss is indefinite or particular.

But if the universality is posited with respect to the minor term either affirmatively or negatively, a syllogism will not be possible, whether the major premiss is positive or negative, indefinite or particular: e.g. if some B is or is not A, and all C is B. As an example of a positive relation between the extremes take the terms good, state, wisdom: of a negative relation, good, state, ignorance. Again if no C is B, but some B is or is not A or not every B is A, there cannot be a syllogism. Take the terms white, horse, swan: white, horse, raven. The same terms may be taken also if the premiss BA is indefinite.

Nor when the major premiss is universal, whether affirmative or negative, and the minor premiss is negative and particular, can there be a syllogism, whether the minor premiss be indefinite or particular: e.g. if all B is A and some C is not B, or if not all C is B. For the major term may be predicable both of all and of none of the minor, to some of which the middle term cannot be attributed. Suppose the terms are animal, man, white: next take some of the white things of which man is not predicated-swan and snow: animal is predicated of all of the one, but of none of the other. Consequently there cannot be a syllogism. Again let no B be A, but let some C not be B. Take the terms inanimate, man, white: then take some white things of which man is not predicated-swan and snow: the term inanimate is predicated of all of the one, of none of the other.

Further since it is indefinite to say some C is not B, and it is true that some C is not B, whether no C is B, or not all C is B, and since if terms are assumed such that no C is B, no syllogism follows (this has already been stated) it is clear that this arrangement of terms will not afford a syllogism:

161

otherwise one would have been possible with a universal negative minor premiss. A similar proof may also be given if the universal premiss is negative.

Nor can there in any way be a syllogism if both the relations of subject and predicate are particular, either positively or negatively, or the one negative and the other affirmative, or one indefinite and the other definite, or both indefinite. Terms common to all the above are animal, white, horse: animal, white, stone.

It is clear then from what has been said that if there is a syllogism in this figure with a particular conclusion, the terms must be related as we have stated: if they are related otherwise, no syllogism is possible anyhow. It is evident also that all the syllogisms in this figure are perfect (for they are all completed by means of the premisses originally taken) and that all conclusions are proved by this figure, viz. universal and particular, affirmative and negative. Such a figure I call the first.

5

Whenever the same thing belongs to all of one subject, and to none of another, or to all of each subject or to none of either, I call such a figure the second; by middle term in it I mean that which is predicated of both subjects, by extremes the terms of which this is said, by major extreme that which lies near the middle, by minor that which is further away from the middle. The middle term stands outside the extremes, and is first in position. A syllogism cannot be perfect anyhow in this figure, but it may be valid whether the terms are related universally or not.

If then the terms are related universally a syllogism will be possible, whenever the middle belongs to all of one subject and to none of another (it does not matter which has the negative relation), but in no other way. Let M be predicated of no N, but of all O. Since, then, the negative relation is convertible, N will belong to no M: but M was assumed to belong to all O: consequently N will belong to no O. This has already been proved. Again if M belongs to all N, but to no O, then N will belong to no O. For if M belongs to no O, O belongs to no M: but M (as was said) belongs to all N: O then will belong to no N: for the first figure has again been formed. But since the negative relation is convertible, N will belong to no O. Thus it will be the same syllogism that proves both conclusions.

It is possible to prove these results also by reductio ad impossibile.

It is clear then that a syllogism is formed when the terms are so related, but not a perfect syllogism; for necessity is not perfectly established merely from the original premisses; others also are needed.

But if M is predicated of every N and O, there cannot be a syllogism. Terms to illustrate a positive relation between the extremes are substance, animal, man; a negative relation, substance, animal, number-substance being the middle term. Nor is a syllogism possible when M is predicated neither of any N nor of any O. Terms to illustrate a positive relation are line, animal, man: a negative relation, line, animal, stone.

It is clear then that if a syllogism is formed when the terms are universally related, the terms must be related as we stated at the outset: for if they are otherwise related no necessary consequence follows.

If the middle term is related universally to one of the extremes, a particular negative syllogism must result whenever the middle term is related universally to the major whether positively or negatively, and particularly to the minor and in a manner opposite to that of the universal statement: by 'an opposite manner' I mean, if the universal statement is negative, the particular is affirmative: if the universal is affirmative, the particular is negative. For if M belongs to no N, but to some O, it is necessary that N does not belong to some O. For since the negative statement is convertible, N will belong to no M: but M was admitted to belong to some O: therefore N will not belong to some O: for the result is reached by means of the first figure. Again if M belongs to all N, but not to some O, it is necessary that N does not belong to some O: for if N belongs to all O, and M is predicated also of all N, M must belong to all O: but we assumed that M does not belong to some O. And if M belongs to all N but not to all O, we shall conclude that N does not belong to all O: the proof is the same as the above. But if M is predicated of all O, but not of all N, there will be no syllogism. Take the terms animal, substance, raven; animal, white, raven. Nor will there be a conclusion when M is predicated of no O, but of some N. Terms to illustrate a positive relation between the extremes are animal, substance, unit: a negative relation, animal, substance, science.

If then the universal statement is opposed to the particular, we have stated when a syllogism will be possible and when not: but if the premisses are similar in form, I mean both negative or both affirmative, a syllogism will not be possible anyhow. First let them be negative, and let the major premiss be universal, e.g. let M belong to no N, and not to some O. It is possible then for N to belong either to all O or to no O. Terms to illustrate the negative relation are black, snow, animal. But it is not possible to find terms of which the extremes are related positively and universally, if M belongs to some O, and does not belong to some O. For if N belonged to all O, but M to no N, then M would belong to no O: but we assumed that it belongs to some O. In this way then it is not admissible to take terms: our point must be proved from the indefinite nature of the particular statement. For since it is true that M does not belong to some O, even if it belongs to no O, and since if it belongs to no O a syllogism is (as we have seen) not possible, clearly it will not be possible now either.

Again let the premisses be affirmative, and let the major premiss as before be universal, e.g. let M belong to all N and to some O. It is possible then for N to belong to all O or to no O. Terms to illustrate the negative relation are white, swan, stone. But it is not possible to take terms to illustrate the universal affirmative relation, for the reason already stated: the point must be proved from the indefinite nature of the particular statement. But if the minor premiss is universal, and M belongs to no O, and not to some N, it is possible for N to belong either to all O or to no O. Terms for the positive relation are white, animal, raven: for the negative relation, white, stone, raven. If the premisses are affirmative, terms for the negative relation are white, animal, snow; for the positive relation, white, animal, swan. Evidently then, whenever the premisses are similar in form, and one is universal, the other particular, a syllogism can, not be formed anyhow. Nor is one possible if the middle term belongs to some of each of the extremes, or does not belong to some of either, or belongs to some of the one, not to some of the other, or belongs to neither universally, or is related to them indefinitely. Common terms for all the above are white, animal, man: white, animal, inanimate. It is clear then from what has been said that if the terms are related to one another in the way stated, a syllogism results of necessity; and if there is a syllogism, the terms must be so related. But it is evident also that all the syllogisms in this figure are imperfect: for all are made perfect by certain supplementary statements, which either are contained in the terms of necessity or are assumed as hypotheses, i.e. when we prove per impossibile. And it is evident that an affirmative conclusion is not attained by means of this figure, but all are negative, whether universal or particular.

6

But if one term belongs to all, and another to none, of a third, or if both belong to all, or to none, of it, I call such a figure the third; by middle term in it I mean that of which both the predicates are predicated, by extremes I mean the predicates, by the major extreme that which is further from the middle, by the minor that which is nearer to it. The middle term stands outside the extremes, and is last in position. A syllogism cannot be perfect in this figure either, but it may be valid whether the terms are related universally or not to the middle term.

If they are universal, whenever both P and R belong to S, it follows that P will necessarily belong to some R. For, since the affirmative statement is convertible, S will belong to some R: consequently since P belongs to all S, and S to some R, P must belong to some R: for a syllogism in the first figure is produced. It is possible to demonstrate this also per impossibile and by exposition. For if both P and R belong to all S, should one of the Ss, e.g. N, be taken, both P and R will belong to this, and thus P will belong to some R.

If R belongs to all S, and P to no S, there will be a syllogism to prove that P will necessarily not belong to some R. This may be demonstrated in the same way as before by converting the premiss RS. It might be proved also per impossibile, as in the former cases. But if R belongs to no S, P to all S, there will be no syllogism. Terms for the positive relation are animal, horse, man: for the negative relation animal, inanimate, man.

Nor can there be a syllogism when both terms are asserted of no S. Terms for the positive relation are animal, horse, inanimate; for the negative relation man, horse, inanimate-inanimate being the middle term.

It is clear then in this figure also when a syllogism will be possible and when not, if the terms are related universally. For whenever both the terms are affirmative, there will be a syllogism to prove that one extreme belongs to some of the other; but when they are negative, no syllogism will be possible. But when one is negative, the other affirmative, if the major is negative, the minor affirmative, there will be a syllogism to prove that the one extreme does not belong to some of the other: but if the relation is reversed, no syllogism will be possible. If one term is related universally to the middle, the other in part only, when both are affirmative there must be a syllogism, no matter which of the premisses is universal. For if R belongs to all S, P to some S, P must belong to some R. For since the affirmative statement is convertible S will belong to some P: consequently since R belongs to all S, and S to some P, R must also belong to some P: therefore P must belong to some R.

Again if R belongs to some S, and P to all S, P must belong to some R. This may be demonstrated in the same way as the preceding. And it is possible to demonstrate it also per impossibile and by exposition, as in the former cases. But if one term is affirmative, the other negative, and if the affirmative is universal, a syllogism will be possible whenever the minor term is affirmative. For if R belongs to all S, but P does not belong to some S, it is necessary that P does not belong to some R. For if P belongs to all R, and R belongs to all S, then P will belong to all S: but we assumed that it did not. Proof is possible also without reduction ad impossibile, if one of the Ss be taken to which P does not belong.

But whenever the major is affirmative, no syllogism will be possible, e.g. if P belongs to all S and R does not belong to some S. Terms for the universal affirmative relation are animate, man, animal. For the universal negative relation it is not possible to get terms, if R belongs to some S, and does not belong to some S. For if P belongs to all S, and R to some S, then P will belong to some R: but we assumed that it belongs to no R. We must put the matter as before.' Since the expression 'it does not belong to some' is indefinite, it may be used truly of that also which belongs to none. But if R belongs to no S, no syllogism is possible, as has been shown. Clearly then no syllogism will be possible here.

But if the negative term is universal, whenever the major is negative and the minor affirmative there will be a syllogism. For if P belongs to no S, and R belongs to some S, P will not belong to some R: for we shall have the first figure again, if the premiss RS is converted.

But when the minor is negative, there will be no syllogism. Terms for the positive relation are animal, man, wild: for the negative relation, animal, science, wild-the middle in both being the term wild.

Nor is a syllogism possible when both are stated in the negative, but one is universal, the other particular. When the minor is related universally to the middle, take the terms animal, science, wild; animal, man, wild. When the major is related universally to the middle, take as terms for a negative relation raven, snow, white. For a positive relation terms cannot be found, if R belongs to some S, and does not belong to some S. For if P belongs to all R, and R to some S, then P belongs to some S: but we assumed that it belongs to no S. Our point, then, must be proved from the indefinite nature of the particular statement.

Nor is a syllogism possible anyhow, if each of the extremes belongs to some of the middle or does not belong, or one belongs and the other does not to some of the middle, or one belongs to some of the middle, the other not to all, or if the premisses are indefinite. Common terms for all are animal, man, white: animal, inanimate, white.

It is clear then in this figure also when a syllogism will be possible, and when not; and that if the terms are as stated, a syllogism results of necessity, and if there is a syllogism, the terms must be so related. It is clear also that all the syllogisms in this figure are imperfect (for all are made perfect by certain supplementary assumptions), and that it will not be possible to reach a universal conclusion by means of this figure, whether negative or affirmative.

7

It is evident also that in all the figures, whenever a proper syllogism does not result, if both the terms are affirmative or negative nothing necessary follows at all, but if one is affirmative, the other negative, and if the negative is stated universally, a syllogism always results relating the minor to the major term, e.g. if A belongs to all or some B, and B belongs to no C: for if the premisses are converted it is necessary that C does not belong to some A. Similarly also in the other figures: a syllogism always results by means of conversion. It is evident also that the substitution of an indefinite for a particular affirmative will effect the same syllogism in all the figures.

It is clear too that all the imperfect syllogisms are made perfect by means of the first figure. For all are brought to a conclusion either ostensively or per impossibile. In both ways the first figure is formed: if they are made perfect ostensively, because (as we saw) all are brought to a conclusion by means of conversion, and conversion produces the first figure: if they are proved per impossibile, because on the assumption of the false statement the syllogism comes about by means of the first figure, e.g. in the last figure, if A and B belong to all C, it follows that A belongs to some B: for if A belonged to no B, and B belongs to all C, A would belong to no C: but (as we stated) it belongs to all C. Similarly also with the rest.

It is possible also to reduce all syllogisms to the universal syllogisms in the first figure. Those in the second figure are clearly made perfect by these, though not all in the same way; the universal syllogisms are made perfect by converting the negative premiss, each of the particular syllogisms by reductio ad impossibile. In the first figure particular syllogisms are indeed made perfect by themselves, but it is possible also to prove them by means of the second figure, reducing them ad impossibile, e.g. if A belongs to all B, and B to some C, it follows that A belongs to some C. For if it belonged to no C, and belongs to all B, then B will belong to no C: this we know by means of the second figure. Similarly also demonstration will be possible in the case of the negative. For if A belongs to no B, and B belongs to some C, A will not belong to some C: for if it belonged to all C, and belongs to no B, then B will belong to no C: and this (as we saw) is the middle figure. Consequently, since all syllogisms in the middle figure can be reduced to universal syllogisms in the first figure, and since particular syllogisms in the first figure can be reduced to syllogisms in the middle figure, it is clear that particular syllogisms can be reduced to universal syllogisms in the first figure. Syllogisms in the third figure, if the terms are universal, are directly made perfect by means of those syllogisms; but, when one of the premisses is particular, by means of the particular syllogisms in the first figure: and these (we have seen) may be reduced to the universal syllogisms in the first figure: consequently also the particular syllogisms in the third figure may be so reduced. It is clear then that all syllogisms may be reduced to the universal syllogisms in the first figure.

We have stated then how syllogisms which prove that something belongs or does not belong to something else are constituted, both how syllogisms of the same figure are constituted in themselves, and how syllogisms of different figures are related to one another.

...

23

It is clear from what has been said that the syllogisms in these figures are made perfect by means of universal syllogisms in the first figure and are reduced to them. That every syllogism without qualification can be so treated, will be clear presently, when it has been proved that every syllogism is formed through one or other of these figures.

It is necessary that every demonstration and every syllogism should prove either that something belongs or that it does not, and this either universally or in part, and further either ostensively or hypothetically. One sort of hypothetical proof is the reductio ad impossibile. Let us speak first of ostensive syllogisms: for after these have been pointed out the truth of our contention will be clear with regard to those which are proved per impossibile, and in general hypothetically.

If then one wants to prove syllogistically A of B, either as an attribute of it or as not an attribute of it, one must assert something of something else. If now A should be asserted of B, the proposition originally in question will have been assumed. But if A should be asserted of C, but C should not be asserted of anything, nor anything of it, nor anything else of A, no syllogism will be possible. For nothing necessarily follows from the assertion of some one thing concerning some other single thing. Thus we must take another premiss as well. If then A be asserted of something else, or something else of A, or something different of C, nothing prevents a syllogism being formed, but it will not be in relation to B through the premisses taken. Nor when C belongs to something else, and that to something else and so on, no connexion however being made with B, will a syllogism be possible concerning A in its relation to B. For in general we stated that no syllogism can establish the attribution of one thing to another, unless some middle term is taken, which is somehow related to each by way of predication. For the syllogism in general is made out of premisses, and a syllogism referring to this out of premisses with the same reference, and a syllogism relating this to that proceeds through premisses which relate this to that. But it is impossible to take a premiss in reference to B, if we neither affirm nor deny anything of it; or again to take a premiss relating A to B, if we take nothing common, but affirm or deny peculiar attributes of each. So we must take something midway between the two, which will connect the predications, if we are to have a syllogism relating this to that. If then we must take something common in relation to both, and this is possible in three ways (either by predicating A of C, and C of B, or C of both, or both of C), and these are the figures of which we have spoken, it is clear that every syllogism must be made in one or other of these figures. The argument is the same if several middle terms should be necessary to establish the relation to B; for the figure will be the same whether there is one middle term or many.

It is clear then that the ostensive syllogisms are effected by means of the aforesaid figures; these considerations will show that reductiones ad also are effected in the same way. For all who effect an argument per impossibile infer syllogistically what is false, and prove the original conclusion hypothetically when something impossible results from the assumption of its contradictory; e.g. that the diagonal of the square is incommensurate with the side, because odd numbers are equal to evens if it is supposed to be commensurate. One infers syllogistically that odd numbers come out equal to evens, and one proves hypothetically the incommensurability of the diagonal, since a falsehood results through contradicting this. For this we found to be reasoning per impossibile, viz. proving something impossible by means of an hypothesis conceded at the beginning. Consequently, since the falsehood is established in reductions ad impossibile by an ostensive syllogism, and the original conclusion is proved hypothetically, and we have already stated that ostensive syllogisms are effected by means of these figures, it is evident that syllogisms per impossibile also will be made through these figures. Likewise all the other hypothetical syllogisms: for in every case the syllogism leads up to the proposition that is substituted for the original thesis; but the original thesis is reached by means of a concession or some other hypothesis. But if this is true, every demonstration and every syllogism must be formed by means of the three figures mentioned above. But when this has been shown it is clear that every syllogism is perfected by means of the first figure and is reducible to the universal syllogisms in this figure.

24

Further in every syllogism one of the premisses must be affirmative, and universality must be present: unless one of the premisses is universal either a syllogism will not be possible, or it will not refer to the subject proposed, or the original position will be begged. Suppose we have to prove that pleasure in music is good. If one should claim as a premiss that pleasure is good without adding 'all', no syllogism will be possible; if one should claim that some pleasure is good, then if it is different from pleasure in music, it is not relevant to the subject proposed; if it is this very pleasure, one is assuming that which was proposed at the outset to be proved. This is more obvious in geometrical proofs, e.g. that the angles at the base of an isosceles triangle are equal. Suppose the lines A and B have been drawn to the centre. If then one should assume that the angle AC is equal to the angle BD, without claiming generally that angles of semicircles are equal; and again if one should assume that the angle C is equal to the angle D, without the additional assumption that every angle of a segment is equal to every other angle of the same segment; and further if one should assume that when equal angles are taken from the whole angles, which are themselves equal, the remainders E and F are equal, he will beg the thing to be proved, unless he also states that when equals are taken from equals the remainders are equal.

It is clear then that in every syllogism there must be a universal premiss, and that a universal statement is proved only when all the premisses are universal, while a particular statement is proved both from two universal premisses and from one only: consequently if the conclusion is universal, the premisses also must be universal, but if the premisses are universal it is possible that the conclusion may not be universal. And it is clear also that in every syllogism either both or one of the premisses must be like the conclusion. I mean not only in being affirmative or negative, but also in being necessary, pure, problematic. We must consider also the other forms of predication.

It is clear also when a syllogism in general can be made and when it cannot; and when a valid, when a perfect syllogism can be formed; and that if a syllogism is formed the terms must be arranged in one of the ways that have been mentioned.

25

It is clear too that every demonstration will proceed through three terms and no more, unless the same conclusion is established by different pairs of propositions; e.g. the conclusion E may be established through the propositions A and B, and through the propositions C and D, or through the propositions A and B, or A and C, or B and C. For nothing prevents there being several middles for the same terms. But in that case there is not one but several syllogisms. Or again when each of the propositions A and B is obtained by syllogistic inference, e.g. by means of D and E, and again B by means of F and G. Or one may be obtained by syllogistic, the other by inductive inference. But thus also the syllogisms are many; for the conclusions are many, e.g. A and B and C. But if this can be called one syllogism, not many, the same conclusion may be reached by more than three terms in this way, but it cannot be reached as C is established by means of A and B. Suppose that the proposition E is inferred from the premisses A, B, C, and D. It is necessary then that of these one should be related to another as whole to part: for it has already been proved that if a syllogism is formed some of its terms must be related in this way. Suppose then that A stands in this relation to B. Some conclusion then follows from them. It must either be E or one or other of C and D, or something other than these.

(1) If it is E the syllogism will have A and B for its sole premisses. But if C and D are so related that one is whole, the other part, some conclusion will follow from them also; and it must be either E, or one or other of the propositions A and B, or something other than these. And if it is (i) E, or (ii) A or B, either (i) the syllogisms will be more than one, or (ii) the same thing happens to be inferred by means of several terms only in the sense which we saw to be possible. But if (iii) the conclusion is other than E or A or B, the syllogisms will be many, and unconnected with one another. But if C is not so related to D as to make a syllogism, the propositions will have been assumed to no purpose, unless for the sake of induction or of obscuring the argument or something of the sort.

(2) But if from the propositions A and B there follows not E but some other conclusion, and if from C and D either A or B follows or something else, then there are several syllogisms, and they do not establish the conclusion proposed: for we assumed that the syllogism proved E. And if no conclusion follows from C and D, it turns out that these propositions have been assumed to no purpose, and the syllogism does not prove the original proposition.

So it is clear that every demonstration and every syllogism will proceed through three terms only.

This being evident, it is clear that a syllogistic conclusion follows from two premisses and not from more than two. For the three terms make two premisses, unless a new premiss is assumed, as was said at the beginning, to perfect the syllogisms. It is clear therefore that in whatever syllogistic argument the premisses through which the main conclusion follows (for some of the preceding conclusions must be premisses) are not even in number, this argument either has not been drawn syllogistically or it has assumed more than was necessary to establish its thesis.

If then syllogisms are taken with respect to their main premisses, every syllogism will consist of an even number of premisses and an odd number of terms (for the terms exceed the premisses by one), and the conclusions will be half the number of the premisses. But whenever a conclusion is reached by means of prosyllogisms or by means of several continuous middle terms, e.g. the proposition AB by means of the middle terms C and D, the number of the terms will similarly exceed that of the premisses by one (for the extra term must either be added outside or inserted: but in either case it follows that the relations of predication are one fewer than the terms related), and the premisses will be equal in number to the relations of predication. The premisses however will not always be even, the terms odd; but they will alternate-when the premisses are even, the terms must be odd; when the terms are even, the premisses must be odd: for along with one term one premiss is added, if a term is added from any quarter. Consequently since the premisses were (as we saw) even, and the terms odd, we must make them alternately even and odd at each addition. But the conclusions will not follow the same arrangement either in respect to the terms or to the premisses. For if one term is added, conclusions will be added less by one than the pre-existing terms: for the conclusion is drawn not in relation to the single term last added, but in relation to all the rest, e.g. if to ABC the term D is added, two conclusions are thereby added, one in relation to A, the other in relation to B. Similarly with any further additions. And similarly too if the term is inserted in the middle: for in relation to one term only, a syllogism will not be constructed. Consequently the conclusions will be much more numerous than the terms or the premisses.

26

Since we understand the subjects with which syllogisms are concerned, what sort of conclusion is established in each figure, and in how many moods this is done, it is evident to us both what sort of problem is difficult and what sort is easy to prove. For that which is concluded in many figures and through many moods is easier; that which is concluded in few figures and through few moods is more difficult to attempt. The universal affirmative is proved by means of the first figure only and by this in only one mood; the universal negative is proved both through the first figure and through the second, through the first in one mood, through the second in two. The particular affirmative is proved through the first and through the last figure, in one mood through the first, in three moods through the last. The particular negative is proved in all the figures, but once in the first, in two moods in the second, in three moods in the third. It is clear then that the universal affirmative is most difficult to establish, most easy to overthrow. In general, universals are easier game for the destroyer than particulars: for whether the predicate belongs to none or not to some, they are destroyed: and the particular negative is proved in all the figures, the universal negative in two. Similarly with universal negatives: the original statement is destroyed, whether the predicate belongs to all or to some: and this we found possible in two figures. But particular statements can be refuted in one way only-by proving that the predicate belongs either to all or to none. But particular statements are easier to establish: for proof is possible in more figures and through more moods. And in general we must not forget that it is possible to refute statements by means of one another, I mean, universal statements by means of particular, and particular statements by means of universal: but it is not possible to establish universal statements by means of particular, though it is possible to establish particular statements by means of universal. At the same time it is evident that it is easier to refute than to establish.

The manner in which every syllogism is produced, the number of the terms and premisses through which it proceeds, the relation of the premisses to one another, the character of the problem proved in each figure, and the number of the figures appropriate to each problem, all these matters are clear from what has been said.

27

We must now state how we may ourselves always have a supply of syllogisms in reference to the problem proposed and by what road we may reach the principles relative to the problem: for perhaps we ought not only to investigate the construction of syllogisms, but also to have the power of making them.

Of all the things which exist some are such that they cannot be predicated of anything else truly and universally, e.g. Cleon and Callias, i.e. the individual and sensible, but other things may be predicated of them (for each of these is both man and animal); and some things are themselves predicated of others, but nothing prior is predicated of them; and some are predicated of others, and yet others of them, e.g. man of Callias and animal of man. It is clear then that some things are naturally not stated of anything: for as a rule each sensible thing is such that it cannot be predicated of anything, save incidentally: for we sometimes say that that white object is Socrates, or that that which approaches is Callias. We shall explain in another place that there is an upward limit also to the process of predicating: for the present we must assume this. Of these ultimate predicates it is not possible to demonstrate another predicate, save as a matter of opinion, but these may be predicated of other things. Neither can individuals be predicated of other things, though other things can be predicated of them. Whatever lies between these limits can be spoken of in both ways: they may be stated of others, and others stated of them. And as a rule arguments and inquiries are concerned with these things. We must select the premisses suitable to each problem in this manner: first we must lay down the subject and the definitions and the properties of the thing; next we must lay down those attributes which follow the thing, and again those which the thing follows, and those which cannot belong to it. But those to which it cannot belong need not be selected, because the negative statement implied above is convertible. Of the attributes which follow we must distinguish those which fall within the definition, those which are predicated as properties, and those which are predicated as accidents, and of the latter those which apparently and those which really belong. The larger the supply a man has of these, the more quickly will he reach a conclusion; and in proportion as he apprehends those which are truer, the more cogently will he demonstrate. But he must select not those which follow some particular but those which follow the thing as a whole, e.g. not what follows a particular man but what follows every man: for the syllogism proceeds through universal premisses. If the statement is indefinite, it is uncertain whether the premiss is universal, but if the statement is definite, the matter is clear. Similarly one must select those attributes which the subject follows as wholes, for the reason given. But that which follows one must not suppose to follow as a whole, e.g. that every animal follows man or every science music, but only that it follows, without qualification, and indeed we state it in a proposition: for the other statement is useless and impossible, e.g. that every man is every animal or justice is all good. But that which something follows receives the mark 'every'. Whenever the subject, for which we must obtain the attributes that follow, is contained by something else, what follows or does not follow the highest term universally must not be selected in dealing with the subordinate term (for these attributes have been taken in dealing with the superior term; for what follows animal also follows man, and what does not belong to animal does not belong to man); but we must choose those attributes which are peculiar to each subject. For some things are peculiar to the species as distinct from the genus; for species being distinct there must be attributes peculiar to each. Nor must we take as things which the superior term follows, those things which the inferior term follows, e.g. take as subjects of the predicate 'animal' what are really subjects of the predicate 'man'. It is necessary indeed, if animal follows man, that it should follow all these also. But these belong more properly to the choice of what concerns man. One must apprehend also normal consequents and normal antecedents-, for propositions which obtain normally are established syllogistically from premisses which obtain normally, some if not all of them having this character of normality. For the conclusion of each syllogism resembles its principles. We must not however choose attributes which are consequent upon all the terms: for no syllogism can be made out of such premisses. The reason why this is so will be clear in the sequel.

...

32

Our next business is to state how we can reduce syllogisms to the aforementioned figures: for this part of the inquiry still remains. If we should investigate the production of the syllogisms and had the power of discovering them, and further if we could resolve the syllogisms produced into the aforementioned figures, our original problem would be brought to a conclusion. It will happen at the same time that what has been already said will be confirmed and its truth made clearer by what we are about to say. For everything that is true must in every respect agree with itself First then we must attempt to select the two premisses of the syllogism (for it is easier to divide into large parts than into small, and the composite parts are larger than the elements out of which they are made); next we must inquire which are universal and which particular, and if both premisses have not been stated, we must ourselves assume the one which is missing. For sometimes men put forward the universal premiss, but do not posit the premiss which is contained in it, either in writing or in discussion: or men put forward the premisses of the principal syllogism, but omit those through which they are inferred, and invite the concession of others to no purpose. We must inquire then whether anything unnecessary has been assumed, or anything necessary has been omitted, and we must posit the one and take away the other, until we have reached the two premisses: for unless we have these, we cannot reduce arguments put forward in the way described. In some arguments it is easy to see what is wanting, but some escape us, and appear to be syllogisms, because something necessary results from what has been laid down, e.g. if the assumptions were made that substance is not annihilated by the annihilation of what is not substance, and that if the elements out of which a thing is made are annihilated, then that which is made out of them is destroyed: these propositions being laid down, it is necessary that any part of substance is substance; this has not however been drawn by syllogism from the propositions assumed, but premisses are wanting. Again if it is necessary that animal should exist, if man does, and that substance should exist, if animal does, it is necessary that substance should exist if man does: but as yet the conclusion has not been drawn syllogistically: for the premisses are not in the shape we required. We are deceived in such cases because something necessary results from what is assumed, since the syllogism also is necessary. But that which is necessary is wider than the syllogism: for every syllogism is necessary, but not everything which is necessary is a syllogism. Consequently, though something results when certain propositions are assumed, we must not try to reduce it directly, but must first state the two premisses, then divide them into their terms. We must take that term as middle which is stated in both the remisses: for it is necessary that the middle should be found in both premisses in all the figures.

If then the middle term is a predicate and a subject of predication, or if it is a predicate, and something else is denied of it, we shall have the first figure: if it both is a predicate and is denied of something, the middle figure: if other things are predicated of it, or one is denied, the other predicated, the last figure. For it was thus that we found the middle term placed in each figure. It is placed similarly too if the premisses are not universal: for the middle term is determined in the same way. Clearly then, if the same term is not stated more than once in the course of an argument, a syllogism cannot be made: for a middle term has not been taken. Since we know what sort of thesis is established in each figure, and in which the universal, in what sort the particular is described, clearly we must not look for all the figures, but for that which is appropriate to the thesis in hand. If the thesis is established in more figures than one, we shall recognize the figure by the position of the middle term.

...

36

That the first term belongs to the middle, and the middle to the extreme, must not be understood in the sense that they can always be predicated of one another or that the first term will be predicated of the middle in the same way as the middle is predicated of the last term. The same holds if the premisses are negative. But we must suppose the verb 'to belong' to have as many meanings as the senses in which the verb 'to be' is used, and in which the assertion that a thing 'is' may be said to be true. Take for example the statement that there is a single science of contraries. Let A stand for 'there being a single science', and B for things which are contrary to one another. Then A belongs to B, not in the sense that contraries are the fact of there being a single science of them, but in the sense that it is true to say of the contraries that there is a single science of them.

It happens sometimes that the first term is stated of the middle, but the middle is not stated of the third term, e.g. if wisdom is knowledge, and wisdom is of the good, the conclusion is that there is knowledge of the good. The good then is not knowledge, though wisdom is knowledge. Sometimes the middle term is stated of the third, but the first is not stated of the middle, e.g. if there is a science of everything that has a quality, or is a contrary, and the good both is a contrary and has a quality, the conclusion is that there is a science of the good, but the good is not science, nor is that which has a quality or is a contrary, though the good is both of these. Sometimes neither the first term is stated of the middle, nor the middle of the third, while the first is sometimes stated of the third, and sometimes not: e.g. if there is a genus of that of which there is a science, and if there is a science of the good, we conclude that there is a genus of the good. But nothing is predicated of anything. And if that of which there is a science is a genus, and if there is a science of the good, we conclude that the good is a genus. The first term then is predicated of the extreme, but in the premisses one thing is not stated of another.

The same holds good where the relation is negative. For 'that does not belong to this' does not always mean that 'this is not that', but sometimes that 'this is not of that' or 'for that', e.g. 'there is not a motion of a motion or a becoming of a becoming, but there is a becoming of pleasure: so pleasure is not a becoming.' Or again it may be said that there is a sign of laughter, but there is not a sign of a sign, consequently laughter is not a sign. This holds in the other cases too, in which the thesis is refuted because the genus is asserted in a particular way, in relation to the terms of the thesis. Again take the inference 'opportunity is not the right time: for opportunity belongs to God, but the right time does not, since nothing is useful to God'. We must take as terms opportunity-right time-God: but the premiss must be understood according to the case of the noun. For we state this universally without qualification, that the terms ought always to be stated in the nominative, e.g. man, good, contraries, not in oblique cases, e.g. of man, of a good, of contraries, but the premisses ought to be understood with reference to the cases of each term-either the dative, e.g. 'equal to this', or the genitive, e.g. 'double of this', or the accusative, e.g. 'that which strikes or sees this', or the nominative, e.g. 'man is an animal', or in whatever other way the word falls in the premiss.

37

The expressions 'this belongs to that' and 'this holds true of that' must be understood in as many ways as there are different categories, and these categories must be taken either with or without qualification, and further as simple or compound: the same holds good of the corresponding negative expressions. We must consider these points and define them better.

38

A term which is repeated in the premisses ought to be joined to the first extreme, not to the middle. I mean for example that if a syllogism should be made proving that there is knowledge of justice, that it is good, the expression 'that it is good' (or 'qua good') should be joined to the first term. Let A stand for 'knowledge that it is good', B for good, C for justice. It is true to predicate A of B. For of the good there is knowledge that it is good. Also it is true to predicate B of C. For justice is identical with a good. In this way an analysis of the argument can be made. But if the expression 'that it is good' were added to B, the conclusion will not follow: for A will be true of B, but B will not be true of C. For to predicate of justice the term 'good that it is good' is false and not intelligible. Similarly if it should be proved that the healthy is an object of knowledge qua good, of goat-stag an object of knowledge qua not existing, or man perishable qua an object of sense: in every case in which an addition is made to the predicate, the addition must be joined to the extreme.

The position of the terms is not the same when something is established without qualification and when it is qualified by some attribute or condition, e.g. when the good is proved to be an object of knowledge and when it is proved to be an object of knowledge that it is good. If it has been proved to be an object of knowledge without qualification, we must put as middle term 'that which is', but if we add the qualification 'that it is good', the middle term must be 'that which is something'. Let A stand for 'knowledge that it is something', B stand for 'something', and C stand for 'good'. It is true to predicate A of B: for ex hypothesi there is a science of that which is something, that it is something. B too is true of C: for that which C represents is something. Consequently A is true of C: there will then be knowledge of the good, that it is good: for ex hypothesi the term 'something' indicates the thing's special nature. But if 'being' were taken as middle and 'being' simply were joined to the extreme, not 'being something', we should not have had a syllogism proving that there is knowledge of the good, that it is good, but that it is; e.g. let A stand for knowledge that it is, B for being, C for good. Clearly then in syllogisms which are thus limited we must take the terms in the way stated.

39

We ought also to exchange terms which have the same value, word for word, and phrase for phrase, and word and phrase, and always take a word in preference to a phrase: for thus the setting out of the terms will be easier. For example if it makes no difference whether we say that the supposable is not the genus of the opinable or that the opinable is not identical with a particular kind of supposable (for what is meant is the same in both statements), it is better to take as the terms the supposable and the opinable in preference to the phrase suggested.

40

Since the expressions 'pleasure is good' and 'pleasure is the good' are not identical, we must not set out the terms in the same way; but if the syllogism is to prove that pleasure is the good, the term must be 'the good', but if the object is to prove that pleasure is good, the term will be 'good'. Similarly in all other cases.

41

It is not the same, either in fact or in speech, that A belongs to all of that to which B belongs, and that A belongs to all of that to all of which B belongs: for nothing prevents B from belonging to C, though not to all C: e.g. let B stand for beautiful, and C for white. If beauty belongs to something white, it is true to say that beauty belongs to that which is white; but not perhaps to everything that is white. If then A belongs to B, but not to everything of which B is predicated, then whether B belongs to all C or merely belongs to C, it is not necessary that A should belong, I do not say to all C, but even to C at all. But if A belongs to everything of which B is truly stated, it will follow that A can be said of all of that of all of which B is said. If however A is said of that of all of which B may be said, nothing prevents B belonging to C, and yet A not belonging to all C or to any C at all. If then we take three terms it is clear that the expression 'A is said of all of which B is said' means this, 'A is said of all the things of which B is said'. And if B is said of all of a third term, so also is A: but if B is not said of all of the third term, there is no necessity that A should be said of all of it.

We must not suppose that something absurd results through setting out the terms: for we do not use the existence of this particular thing, but imitate the geometrician who says that 'this line a foot long' or 'this straight line' or 'this line without breadth' exists although it does not, but does not use the diagrams in the sense that he reasons from them. For in general, if two things are not related as whole to part and part to whole, the prover does not prove from them, and so no syllogism a is formed. We (I mean the learner) use the process of setting out terms like perception by sense, not as though it were impossible to demonstrate without these illustrative terms, as it is to demonstrate without the premisses of the syllogism.

42

We should not forget that in the same syllogism not all conclusions are reached through one figure, but one through one figure, another through another. Clearly then we must analyse arguments in accordance with this. Since not every problem is proved in every figure, but certain problems in each figure, it is clear from the conclusion in what figure the premisses should be sought.

43

In reference to those arguments aiming at a definition which have been directed to prove some part of the definition, we must take as a term the point to which the argument has been directed, not the whole definition: for so we shall be less likely to be disturbed by the length of the term: e.g. if a man proves that water is a drinkable liquid, we must take as terms drinkable and water.

44

Further we must not try to reduce hypothetical syllogisms; for with the given premisses it is not possible to reduce them. For they have not been proved by syllogism, but assented to by agreement. For instance if a man should

Reasoning

suppose that unless there is one faculty of contraries, there cannot be one science, and should then argue that not every faculty is of contraries, e.g. of what is healthy and what is sickly: for the same thing will then be at the same time healthy and sickly. He has shown that there is not one faculty of all contraries, but he has not proved that there is not a science. And yet one must agree. But the agreement does not come from a syllogism, but from an hypothesis. This argument cannot be reduced: but the proof that there is not a single faculty can. The latter argument perhaps was a syllogism: but the former was an hypothesis.

The same holds good of arguments which are brought to a conclusion per impossibile. These cannot be analysed either; but the reduction to what is impossible can be analysed since it is proved by syllogism, though the rest of the argument cannot, because the conclusion is reached from an hypothesis. But these differ from the previous arguments: for in the former a preliminary agreement must be reached if one is to accept the conclusion; e.g. an agreement that if there is proved to be one faculty of contraries, then contraries fall under the same science; whereas in the latter, even if no preliminary agreement has been made, men still accept the reasoning, because the falsity is patent, e.g. the falsity of what follows from the assumption that the diagonal is commensurate, viz. that then odd numbers are equal to evens.

Many other arguments are brought to a conclusion by the help of an hypothesis; these we ought to consider and mark out clearly. We shall describe in the sequel their differences, and the various ways in which hypothetical arguments are formed: but at present this much must be clear, that it is not

192

possible to resolve such arguments into the figures. And we have explained the reason.

45

Whatever problems are proved in more than one figure, if they have been established in one figure by syllogism, can be reduced to another figure, e.g. a negative syllogism in the first figure can be reduced to the second, and a syllogism in the middle figure to the first, not all however but some only. The point will be clear in the sequel. If A belongs to no B, and B to all C, then A belongs to no C. Thus the first figure; but if the negative statement is converted, we shall have the middle figure. For B belongs to no A, and to all C. Similarly if the syllogism is not universal but particular, e.g. if A belongs to no B, and B to some C. Convert the negative statement and you will have the middle figure.

The universal syllogisms in the second figure can be reduced to the first, but only one of the two particular syllogisms. Let A belong to no B and to all C. Convert the negative statement, and you will have the first figure. For B will belong to no A and A to all C. But if the affirmative statement concerns B, and the negative C, C must be made first term. For C belongs to no A, and A to all B: therefore C belongs to no B. B then belongs to no C: for the negative statement is convertible.

But if the syllogism is particular, whenever the negative statement concerns the major extreme, reduction to the first figure will be possible, e.g. if A belongs to no B and to some C: convert the negative statement and you will have the first figure. For B will belong to no A and A to some C. But when the affirmative statement concerns the major extreme, no resolution will be possible, e.g. if A belongs to all B, but not to all C: for the statement AB does not admit of conversion, nor would there be a syllogism if it did.

Again syllogisms in the third figure cannot all be resolved into the first, though all syllogisms in the first figure can be resolved into the third. Let A belong to all B and B to some C. Since the particular affirmative is convertible, C will belong to some B: but A belonged to all B: so that the third figure is formed. Similarly if the syllogism is negative: for the particular affirmative is convertible: therefore A will belong to no B, and to some C.

Of the syllogisms in the last figure one only cannot be resolved into the first, viz. when the negative statement is not universal: all the rest can be resolved. Let A and B be affirmed of all C: then C can be converted partially with either A or B: C then belongs to some B. Consequently we shall get the first figure, if A belongs to all C, and C to some of the Bs. If A belongs to all C and B to some C, the argument is the same: for B is convertible in reference to C. But if B belongs to all C and A to some C, the first term must be B: for B belongs to all C, and C to some A, therefore B belongs to some A. But since the particular statement is convertible, A will belong to some B. If the syllogism is negative, when the terms are universal we must take them in a similar way. Let B belong to all C, and A to no C: then C will belong to some B, and A to no C; and so C will be middle term. Similarly if the negative statement is universal, the affirmative particular: for A will belong to no C, and C to some of the Bs. But if the negative statement is particular, no resolution will be possible, e.g. if B belongs to all C, and A not belong to some C: convert the statement BC and both premisses will be particular.

It is clear that in order to resolve the figures into one another the premiss which concerns the minor extreme must be converted in both the figures: for when this premiss is altered, the transition to the other figure is made.

One of the syllogisms in the middle figure can, the other cannot, be resolved into the third figure. Whenever the universal statement is negative, resolution is possible. For if A belongs to no B and to some C, both B and C alike are convertible in relation to A, so that B belongs to no A and C to some A. A therefore is middle term. But when A belongs to all B, and not to some C, resolution will not be possible: for neither of the premisses is universal after conversion.

Syllogisms in the third figure can be resolved into the middle figure, whenever the negative statement is universal, e.g. if A belongs to no C, and B to some or all C. For C then will belong to no A and to some B. But if the negative statement is particular, no resolution will be possible: for the particular negative does not admit of conversion.

It is clear then that the same syllogisms cannot be resolved in these figures which could not be resolved into the first figure, and that when syllogisms are reduced to the first figure these alone are confirmed by reduction to what is impossible.

It is clear from what we have said how we ought to reduce syllogisms, and that the figures may be resolved into one another.

Part II

We have already explained the number of the figures, the character and number of the premisses, when and how a syllogism is formed; further what we must look for when a refuting and establishing propositions, and how we should investigate a given problem in any branch of inquiry, also by what means we shall obtain principles appropriate to each subject. Since some syllogisms are universal, others particular, all the universal syllogisms give more than one result, and of particular syllogisms the affirmative yield more than one, the negative yield only the stated conclusion. For all propositions are convertible save only the particular negative: and the conclusion states one definite thing about another definite thing. Consequently all syllogisms save the particular negative yield more than one conclusion, e.g. if A has been proved to to all or to some B, then B must belong to some A: and if A has been proved to belong to no B, then B belongs to no A. This is a different conclusion from the former. But if A does not belong to some B, it is not necessary that B should not belong to some A: for it may possibly belong to all A.

This then is the reason common to all syllogisms whether universal or particular. But it is possible to give another reason concerning those which are universal. For all the things that are subordinate to the middle term or to the conclusion may be proved by the same syllogism, if the former are placed in the middle, the latter in the conclusion; e.g. if the conclusion AB is proved through C, whatever is subordinate to B or C must accept the predicate A: for if D is included in B as in a whole, and B is included in A, then D will be included in A. Again if E is included in C as in a

196

whole, and C is included in A, then E will be included in A. Similarly if the syllogism is negative. In the second figure it will be possible to infer only that which is subordinate to the conclusion, e.g. if A belongs to no B and to all C; we conclude that B belongs to no C. If then D is subordinate to C, clearly B does not belong to it. But that B does not belong to what is subordinate to A is not clear by means of the syllogism. And yet B does not belong to E, if E is subordinate to A. But while it has been proved through the syllogism that B belongs to no C, it has been assumed without proof that B does not belong to A, consequently it does not result through the syllogism that B does not belong to E.

But in particular syllogisms there will be no necessity of inferring what is subordinate to the conclusion (for a syllogism does not result when this premiss is particular), but whatever is subordinate to the middle term may be inferred, not however through the syllogism, e.g. if A belongs to all B and B to some C. Nothing can be inferred about that which is subordinate to C; something can be inferred about that which is subordinate to B, but not through the preceding syllogism. Similarly in the other figures. That which is subordinate to the conclusion cannot be proved; the other subordinate can be proved, only not through the syllogism, just as in the universal syllogisms what is subordinate to the middle term is proved (as we saw) from a premiss which is not demonstrated: consequently either a conclusion is not possible in the case of universal syllogisms or else it is possible also in the case of particular syllogisms.

...

197

8

To convert a syllogism means to alter the conclusion and make another syllogism to prove that either the extreme cannot belong to the middle or the middle to the last term. For it is necessary, if the conclusion has been changed into its opposite and one of the premisses stands, that the other premiss should be destroyed. For if it should stand, the conclusion also must stand. It makes a difference whether the conclusion is converted into its contradictory or into its contrary. For the same syllogism does not result whichever form the conversion takes. This will be made clear by the sequel. By contradictory opposition I mean the opposition of 'to all' to 'not to all', and of 'to some' to 'to none'; by contrary opposition I mean the opposition of 'to all' to 'to none', and of 'to some' to 'not to some'. Suppose that A been proved of C, through B as middle term. If then it should be assumed that A belongs to no C, but to all B, B will belong to no C. And if A belongs to no C, and B to all C, A will belong, not to no B at all, but not to all B. For (as we saw) the universal is not proved through the last figure. In a word it is not possible to refute universally by conversion the premiss which concerns the major extreme: for the refutation always proceeds through the third since it is necessary to take both premisses in reference to the minor extreme. Similarly if the syllogism is negative. Suppose it has been proved that A belongs to no C through B. Then if it is assumed that A belongs to all C, and to no B, B will belong to none of the Cs. And if A and B belong to all C, A will belong to some B: but in the original premiss it belonged to no B.

If the conclusion is converted into its contradictory, the syllogisms will be contradictory and not universal. For one premiss is particular, so that the conclusion also will be particular. Let the syllogism be affirmative, and let it be converted as stated. Then if A belongs not to all C, but to all B, B will belong not to all C. And if A belongs not to all C, but B belongs to all C, A will belong not to all B. Similarly if the syllogism is negative. For if A belongs to some C, and to no B, B will belong, not to no C at all, but-not to some C. And if A belongs to some C, and B to all C, as was originally assumed, A will belong to some B.

In particular syllogisms when the conclusion is converted into its contradictory, both premisses may be refuted, but when it is converted into its contrary, neither. For the result is no longer, as in the universal syllogisms, refutation in which the conclusion reached by O, conversion lacks universality, but no refutation at all. Suppose that A has been proved of some C. If then it is assumed that A belongs to no C, and B to some C, A will not belong to some B: and if A belongs to no C, but to all B, B will belong to no C. Thus both premisses are refuted. But neither can be refuted if the conclusion is converted into its contrary. For if A does not belong to some C, but to all B, then B will not belong to some C. But the original premiss is not yet refuted: for it is possible that B should belong to some C, and should not belong to some C. The universal premiss AB cannot be affected by a syllogism at all: for if A does not belong to some of the Cs, but B belongs to some of the Cs, neither of the premisses is universal. Similarly if the syllogism is negative: for if it should be assumed that A belongs to all C, both premisses are refuted: but if the assumption is that A belongs to some C, neither premiss is refuted. The proof is the same as before.

...

18

A false argument depends on the first false statement in it. Every syllogism is made out of two or more premisses. If then the false conclusion is drawn from two premisses, one or both of them must be false: for (as we proved) a false syllogism cannot be drawn from two premisses. But if the premisses are more than two, e.g. if C is established through A and B, and these through D, E, F, and G, one of these higher propositions must be false, and on this the argument depends: for A and B are inferred by means of D, E, F, and G. Therefore the conclusion and the error results from one of them.

19

In order to avoid having a syllogism drawn against us we must take care, whenever an opponent asks us to admit the reason without the conclusions, not to grant him the same term twice over in his premisses, since we know that a syllogism cannot be drawn without a middle term, and that term which is stated more than once is the middle. How we ought to watch the middle in reference to each conclusion, is evident from our knowing what kind of thesis is proved in each figure. This will not escape us since we know how we are maintaining the argument.

That which we urge men to beware of in their admissions, they ought in attack to try to conceal. This will be possible first, if, instead of drawing the conclusions of preliminary syllogisms, they take the necessary premisses and leave the conclusions in the dark; secondly if instead of inviting assent to propositions which are closely connected they take as far as possible those that are not connected by middle terms. For example suppose that A is to be inferred to be true of F, B, C, D, and E being middle terms. One ought then to ask whether A belongs to B, and next whether D belongs to E, instead of asking whether B belongs to C; after that he may ask whether B belongs to C, and so on. If the syllogism is drawn through one middle term, he ought to begin with that: in this way he will most likely deceive his opponent.

20

Since we know when a syllogism can be formed and how its terms must be related, it is clear when refutation will be possible and when impossible. A refutation is possible whether everything is conceded, or the answers alternate (one, I mean, being affirmative, the other negative). For as has been shown a syllogism is possible whether the terms are related in affirmative propositions or one proposition is affirmative, the other negative: consequently, if what is laid down is contrary to the conclusion, a refutation must take place: for a refutation is a syllogism which establishes the contradictory. But if nothing is conceded, a refutation is impossible: for no syllogism is possible (as we saw) when all the terms are negative: therefore no refutation is possible. For if a refutation were possible, a syllogism must be possible; although if a syllogism is possible it does not follow that a refutation is possible. Similarly refutation is not possible if nothing is conceded universally: since the fields of refutation and syllogism are defined in the same way.

21

It sometimes happens that just as we are deceived in the arrangement of the terms, so error may arise in our thought about them, e.g. if it is possible that the same predicate should belong to more than one subject immediately, but although knowing the one, a man may forget the other and think the opposite true. Suppose that A belongs to B and to C in virtue of their nature, and that B and C belong to all D in the same way. If then a man thinks that A belongs to all B, and B to D, but A to no C, and C to all D, he will both know and not know the same thing in respect of the same thing. Again if a man were to make a mistake about the members of a single series; e.g. suppose A belongs to B, B to C, and C to D, but some one thinks that A belongs to all B, but to no C: he will both know that A belongs to D, and think that it does not. Does he then maintain after this simply that what he knows, he does not think? For he knows in a way that A belongs to C through B, since the part is included in the whole; so that what he knows in a way, this he maintains he does not think at all: but that is impossible.

In the former case, where the middle term does not belong to the same series, it is not possible to think both the premisses with reference to each of the two middle terms: e.g. that A belongs to all B, but to no C, and both B and C belong to all D. For it turns out that the first premiss of the one syllogism is either wholly or partially contrary to the first premiss of the other. For if he thinks that A belongs to everything to which B belongs, and he knows that B belongs to D, then he knows that A belongs to D. Consequently if again he thinks that A belongs to nothing to which C belongs, he thinks that A does not belong to some of that to which B belongs; but if he thinks that A belongs to everything to which B belongs, and again thinks that A does not belong to some of that to which B belongs, these beliefs are wholly or partially contrary. In this way then it is not possible to think; but nothing prevents a man thinking one premiss of each syllogism of both premisses of one of the two syllogisms: e.g. A belongs to all B, and B to D, and again A belongs to no C. An error of this kind is similar to the error into which we fall concerning particulars: e.g. if A belongs to all B, and B to all C, A will belong to all C. If then a man knows that A belongs to everything to which B belongs, he knows that A belongs to C. But nothing prevents his being ignorant that C exists; e.g. let A stand for two right angles, B for triangle, C for a particular diagram of a triangle. A man might think that C did not exist, though he knew that every triangle contains two right angles; consequently he will know and not know the same thing at the same time. For the expression 'to know that every triangle has its angles equal to two right angles' is ambiguous, meaning to have the knowledge either of the universal or of the particulars. Thus then he knows that C contains two right angles with a knowledge of the universal, but not with a knowledge of the particulars; consequently his knowledge will not be contrary to his ignorance. The argument in the Meno that learning is recollection may be criticized in a similar way. For it never happens that a man starts with a foreknowledge of the particular, but along with the process of being led to see the general principle he receives a knowledge of the particulars, by an act (as it were) of recognition. For we know some things directly; e.g. that the angles are equal to two right angles, if we know that the figure is a triangle. Similarly in all other cases.

By a knowledge of the universal then we see the particulars, but we do not know them by the kind of knowledge which is proper to them; consequently it is possible that we may make mistakes about them, but not that we should have the knowledge and error that are contrary to one another: rather we have the knowledge of the universal but make a mistake in apprehending the particular. Similarly in the cases stated above. The error in respect of the middle term is not contrary to the knowledge obtained through the syllogism, nor is the thought in respect of one middle term contrary to that in respect of the other. Nothing prevents a man who knows both that A belongs to the whole of B, and that B again belongs to C, thinking that A does not belong to C, e.g. knowing that every mule is sterile and that this is a mule, and thinking that this animal is with foal: for he does not know that A belongs to C, unless he considers the two propositions together. So it is evident that if he knows the one and does not know the other, he will fall into error. And this is the relation of knowledge of the universal to knowledge of the particular. For we know no sensible thing, once it has passed beyond the range of our senses, even if we happen to have perceived it, except by means of the universal and the possession of the knowledge which is proper to the particular, but without the actual exercise of that knowledge. For to know is used in three senses: it may mean either to have knowledge of the universal or to have knowledge proper to the matter in hand or to exercise such knowledge: consequently three kinds of error also are possible. Nothing then prevents a man both knowing and being mistaken about the same thing, provided that his knowledge and his error are not contrary. And this happens also to the man whose knowledge is limited to each of the premisses and who has not previously considered the particular question. For when he thinks that the mule is with foal he has not the knowledge in the sense of its actual exercise, nor on the other hand has his thought caused an error contrary to his knowledge: for the error contrary to the knowledge of the universal would be a syllogism.

But he who thinks the essence of good is the essence of bad will think the same thing to be the essence of good and the essence of bad. Let A stand for the essence of good and B for the essence of bad, and again C for the essence of good. Since then he thinks B and C identical, he will think that C is B, and similarly that B is A, consequently that C is A. For just as we saw that if B is true of all of which C is true, and A is true of all of which B is true, A is true of C, similarly with the word 'think'. Similarly also with the word 'is'; for we saw that if C is the same as B, and B as A, C is the same as A. Similarly therefore with 'opine'. Perhaps then this is necessary if a man will grant the first point. But presumably that is false, that any one could suppose the essence of good to be the essence of bad, save incidentally. For it is possible to think this in many different ways. But we must consider this matter better.

...

23

It is clear then how the terms are related in conversion, and in respect of being in a higher degree objects of aversion or of desire. We must now state that not only dialectical and demonstrative syllogisms are formed by means of the aforesaid figures, but also rhetorical syllogisms and in general any form of persuasion, however it may be presented. For every belief comes either through syllogism or from induction.

Now induction, or rather the syllogism which springs out of induction, consists in establishing syllogistically a relation between one extreme and the middle by means of the other extreme, e.g. if B is the middle term between A and C, it consists in proving through C that A belongs to B. For this is the manner in which we make inductions. For example let A stand for long-lived, B for bileless, and C for the particular long-lived animals, e.g. man, horse, mule. A then belongs to the whole of C: for whatever is bileless is long-lived. But B also ('not possessing bile') belongs to all C. If then C is convertible with B, and the middle term is not wider in extension, it is necessary that A should belong to B. For it has already been proved that if two things belong to the same thing, and the extreme is convertible with one of them, then the other predicate will belong to the predicate that is converted. But we must apprehend C as made up of all the particulars. For induction proceeds through an enumeration of all the cases.

Such is the syllogism which establishes the first and immediate premiss: for where there is a middle term the syllogism proceeds through the middle term; when there is no middle term, through induction. And in a way induction is opposed to syllogism: for the latter proves the major term to belong to the third term by means of the middle, the former proves the major to belong to the middle by means of the third. In the order of nature, syllogism through the middle term is prior and better known, but syllogism through induction is clearer to us.

...

25

By reduction we mean an argument in which the first term clearly belongs to the middle, but the relation of the middle to the last term is uncertain though equally or more probable than the conclusion; or again an argument in which the terms intermediate between the last term and the middle are few. For in any of these cases it turns out that we approach more nearly to knowledge. For example let A stand for what can be taught, B for knowledge, C for justice. Now it is clear that knowledge can be taught: but it is uncertain whether virtue is knowledge. If now the statement BC is equally or more probable than AC, we have a reduction: for we are nearer to knowledge, since we have taken a new term, being so far without knowledge that A belongs to C. Or again suppose that the terms intermediate between B and C are few: for thus too we are nearer knowledge. For example let D stand for squaring, E for rectilinear figure, F for circle. If there were only one term intermediate between E and F (viz. that the circle is made equal to a rectilinear figure by the help of lunules), we should be near to knowledge. But when BC is not more probable than AC, and the intermediate terms are not few, I do not call this reduction: nor again when the statement BC is immediate: for such a statement is knowledge.

From St. Thomas Aquinas, *Commentary on On Interpretation* I.1:

There is a twofold operation of the intellect, as the Philosopher says in III *De Anima*. One is the understanding of simple objects, that is, the operation by which the intellect apprehends just the essence of a thing alone; the other is the operation of composing and dividing. There is also a third operation, that of reasoning, by which reason proceeds from what is known to the investigation of things that are unknown. The first of these operations is ordered to the second, for there cannot be composition and division unless things have already been apprehended simply. The second, in turn, is ordered to the third, for clearly we must proceed from some known truth to which the intellect assents in order to have certitude about something not yet known.

From St. Thomas Aquinas, *Commentary on Posterior Analytics* I.2:

Since two propositions are needed for inferring a conclusion, namely, a major and a minor; when the major proposition is known, the conclusion is not yet known. Therefore, the major proposition is known before the conclusion not only in nature but in time. Further, if in the minor proposition something is introduced or employed which is contained under the universal proposition which is the major, but it is not evident that it is contained under this universal, then a knowledge of the conclusion is not yet possessed, because the truth of the minor proposition will not yet be certain. But if in the minor proposition a term is taken about which it is clear that it is contained under the universal in the major proposition, the truth of the minor proposition is clear, because that which is taken under the universal shares in the same knowledge, and so the knowledge of the conclusion is had at once.

From John of St. Thomas, *Cursus philosophicus* I.I.8.3:

A syllogism is as it were an organic instrument, which consists of the moving part and of the part moved, just as in living things one part moves another. For it is certain that the premises are the motive and the reason for knowing the conclusion, and thus the premises are necessarily and essentially required for the reason of the syllogism, from which the knowledge of the conclusion arises as if from an instrument. Similarly the conclusion itself is the object known; for the syllogism proceeds in order that the conclusion might be known through the process of inference. The syllogism is a logical tool by which the intellect is moved from one thing to another which is the object to be known, whence it should include the moving part, which constitute the premises, and the part moved, which is the inferred object or conclusion.

From St. Thomas Aquinas, *Commentary on the Ethics*, 1.1:

Order can be related to the reason in four different ways. There is an order which the reason does not make but only considers: such as the order of the things of nature. There is another order which the reason, through its own consideration, brings about in its own act, for instance, when it orders its concepts in relation to each other, and the signs of its concepts, which are significative sounds. In the third place there is the order which the reason, through its consideration, brings about in the operations of the will. In the fourth place, there is the order which the reason, through its consideration, brings about in external things of which it is the cause, e.g., an arch or a house. The order which the reason considers but does not make pertains to natural philosophy; the order which the reason brings about in its own act, through its own consideration, pertains to rational philosophy (viz. logic); the order of the acts of the will pertains to moral philosophy; the order which the reason, through its consideration, brings about in external things, pertains to mechanical arts.

REASONING - COMMENTARY

A **Syllogism** has three propositions:
two **premises** and a **conclusion**.

It contains **three terms**, each used twice:

1. The **Minor Term (S)** is the **Subject** of the **Conclusion**.
   (The **Minor Premise** is the Premise with the Minor Term)

2. The **Major Term (P)** is the **Predicate** of the **Conclusion**.
   (The **Major Premise** is the Premise with the Major Term)

3. The **Middle Term (M)** is the Term not in the Conclusion.

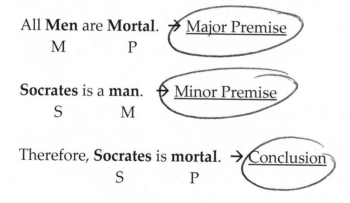

All **Men** are **Mortal.** → Major Premise
   M   P

Socrates is a **man.** → Minor Premise
  S   M

Therefore, **Socrates** is **mortal.** → Conclusion
       S   P

In order for a Conclusion to be TRUE:

- All **Terms** must be CLEAR. (*Simple Apprehension*)

- All **Propositions** must be TRUE. (*Judgment*)

- The Form of the **Syllogism** must be VALID. (*Reasoning*)

Checking the Validity of the Syllogism

Syllogisms have **Mood** and **Figure**:
The **Mood** is the sum of the **three "types"** of its Propositions:

All men are mortal - "A" (Universal Affirmative)
Socrates is a man - "A"
Therefore, Socrates is mortal - "A"
Mood = AAA

The **Figure** of a Syllogism is determined by the location of the **Middle Term**:

Figure 1	Figure 2	Figure 3	Figure 4
M - P	P - **M**	**M** - P	P - **M**
S - **M**	S - **M**	**M** - S	**M** - S
S - P	S - P	S - P	S - P

✳ Aristotle's Six Rules
1. A syllogism must have three and only three terms.
2. A syllogism must have three and only three propositions.
3. The middle term must be distributed at least once.
4. No term that is undistributed in the premise may be distributed in the conclusion.
5. No syllogism can have two negative premises.
6. If one premise is negative, the conclusion must be negative; if the conclusion is negative, one premise must be negative.

Corollary 1. No syllogism may have two particular premises.
Corollary 2. If a syllogism has a particular premise, it must have a particular conclusion.

REDUCTION TO FIRST FIGURE

(Figure 1) - **Barbara, Celarent, Darii, Ferio**
(Figure 2) - **Cesare, Camestres, Festino, Baroco**
(Figure 3) - **Darapti, Felapton, Disamis, Datisi, Bocardo, Ferison**

The meaning of the letters of the above names:
A, E, I, O = The **Mood** of the Syllogism
Example: Barbara = AAA Mood, **C**amestres = AE*E* Mood.

B, C, D, F = The type of **First Figure** Syllogism they reduce to
Example: Cesare reduces to Celarent.

S, P, M, 🐝 = **What should be done** to the PREVIOUS
    proposition to reduce to Figure 1. Doesn't apply to "M"
Example: Cesare - The first "E" Proposition should be
Simply Converted to reduce this syllogism from Cesare (Fig.
2) to Celarent (Fig. 1). See below for Reductions.

R, L, N, T = Nothing.

Figure 1	Figure 2	Figure 3
M - P	P - M	M - P
S - M	S - M	M - S
S - P	S - P	S - P
Barbara - AAA	Cesare - EAE	Darapti - AAI
Celarent - EAE	Camestres - AEE	Felapton - EAO
Darii - AII	Festino - EIO	Disamis - IAI
Ferio - EIO	Baroco - AOO	Datisi - AII
		Bocardo - OAO
		Ferison - EIO

Don't have
to memorize ↙

TYPES OF REDUCTION

S - Simple Conversion
Switch Subject and Predicate. Valid with E and I Propositions.

No snake is a mammal. > No mammal is a snake.

P - Limitation (*Per Accidens*)
Switch Subject and Predicate and limit to a Particular. Valid with A Propositions.

Every mammal is an animal. > Some animals are mammals.

M - Transposition (*Mutatio*)
Switch Major and Minor Premises. Never used alone.

Every wrestler is a tough guy.   No golfer is a tough guy.
No golfer is a tough guy.   > Every wrestler is a tough guy.
Therefore, no golfer is a wrestler. Therefore, no golfer is a wrestler.

C - Contradiction
Contradict the conclusion and switch it with the O Premise. Bocardo & Baroco. This is used only to show that one of the premises must be false.

Every animal is sensible.   Every animal is sensible.
Some stone is not sensible.   >   Every stone is an animal.
Therefore, some stone is not an animal. Therefore, every stone is sensible.

REASONING – SUPPLEMENT

WHETHER NAPS ARE NECESSARY FOR SALVATION

Thus we proceed to the only article: Whether naps are necessary for salvation.

Objection #1
It would seem that naps are not necessary for salvation. Salvation consists in becoming like God. God is the most actual being. Hence, we are meant to be actual beings as well. Now, naps are opposed to actuality and are hence opposed to salvation.

Objection #2
Also, the Apostle says, "Be watchful and awake, for your salvation is near at hand." Naps are opposed to being watchful. Hence, it follows that naps are opposed to salvation.

Objection #3
Furthermore, the Philosopher says that virtue consists in activity. Naps are not activity and are, therefore, not counted as virtuous. Hence, it follows that naps are opposed to salvation.

On the contrary
Sed contra, the Pslamist says, "He pours gifts on his beloved while they slumber." Now, salvation is a gift, and we must sleep to receive the gifts of God. Therefore, naps are necessary for salvation.

I answer that naps can be spoken of in two ways: naps in a relative sense (*secundum quid*) and naps simply speaking (*simpliciter dicta*). Secundum quid, naps are neutral in that they can be used for a good or a bad purpose. Naps, simpliciter dicta, are those naps which give us the rest that we might wake "refreshed and joyful" to praise God (as the Breviary says). To this end naps are necessary for salvation, since praising God is necessary for salvation.

215

Furthermore, contemplation is said to be "rest in God." Now, contemplation flows from Charity, and Charity is necessary for salvation. It follows, therefore, that naps which are also a kind of rest are necessary for salvation. Likewise, contemplation is said to be a foretaste of heavenly beatitude, so naps are a foretaste of heavenly beatitude.

Furthermore, Jesus slept in the boat. Hence, we are to sleep in the Church, for the boat is a type of the Church. We are to sleep even in church, often during homilies.

Consequently, it must be said that naps are necessary for salvation.

Reply to Objection #1

To the first objection, that God is the most actual being, I respond that in God's actuality is all perfection. Hence, God is actually napping.

Reply to Objection #2

To the second objection, that the Apostle admonishes us to be watchful, I respond that he spoke figuratively, not literally. Saint Joseph was watchful in his sleep and that is why God spoke to him in a dream. So also God spoke to many saints in dreams. Hence, we are to nap watchfully, that God might speak to us.

Reply to Objection #3

Finally, in response to the third objection, that the Philosopher says virtue consists in activity, I respond that the Philosopher was a pagan and cannot be expected to have understood the deep mysteries of God's napping. Had he known revelation, he would have napped much more than he did.

Sample Syllogisms

1. All things with a heartbeat are alive. **A**
Dead men are not alive. **E**   *Figure 2*
Therefore, dead men do not have a heartbeat. **E**

2. All bodies are made of parts.
The soul is not made of parts.
Therefore, the soul is not a body.

3. No immaterial thing is made of parts.
Man is made of parts.
Therefore, man is not immaterial.

4. Fools are never blessed. **E**
Some fools are lucky. **I**   *Figure 3*
Therefore, not all lucky people are blessed. **O**

5. No good person is skinny. **E**
Every surfer is skinny. **A**   *Figure 2*
Therefore, no surfer is a good person. **E**

6. Some Detroiters carry a gun.
All Detroiters are in Michigan.
Therefore, some in Michigan carry a gun.

7. Every sailor likes to eat pizza.
Every sailor is on a ship.
Therefore, some on a ship like to eat pizza.

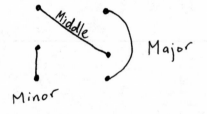

NON-CATEGORICAL SYLLOGISMS

✳ **The Enthymeme**:
A syllogism missing one of the propositions:

John will never get a good job because he didn't graduate.

To formulate a syllogism, find the conclusion, then the major, minor and middle terms:

Those who did not graduate will not get a good job.
John did not graduate.
Therefore, John will not get a good job.

✳ **Sorites** - a series of syllogisms without conclusions.
✳ **Progressive (Aristotelian) Sorites** - First premise contains the Subject:

Every man is an animal.
Every animal is a living thing.
Every living thing is a substance.
Every substance is an existing thing.
Therefore, every man is an existing.

vs.
Every man is an animal.
Every animal is a living thing.
Therefore, every man is a living thing.
etc.

Rules: Only the first premise may be particular, and only the last negative.

✳ **Regressive (Goclenian) Sorites** - First premise contains the Predicate:

Every substance is an existing thing.
Every living thing is a substance.
Every animal is a living thing.
Every man is an animal.
Therefore, every man is an existing thing.

<u>Rules</u>: Only the first premise may be negative, and only the last particular.

✳ **<u>The Epicheirema</u>** - a syllogism with a causal premise (a "double syllogism"):

> *Every doctor is smart because they all study hard.*
> *Lenny is a doctor.*
> *Therefore, Lenny is smart.*

This is actually two syllogisms:

> *Everyone who studies hard is smart.*
> *Doctors study hard.*
> *Therefore, doctors are smart.*
> +
> *Every doctor is smart.*
> *Lenny is a doctor.*
> *Therefore, Lenny is smart.*

✳ **Compound Syllogisms**:

✳ **Conditional Syllogisms** - the first proposition contains an "if...then" statement:

> *If Socrates is eating, then he exists.*
> *Socrates is eating.*
> *Therefore, Socrates exists.*

The antecedent must be affirmed or the consequent denied for the conclusion to be affected. There must be a necessary connection between antecedent and consequent.

✳ **Disjunctive Syllogisms** - the first proposition contains an "either...or" statement:

Strong disjunct (cannot both be true):
> *The number 4 must be either even or odd.*
> *The number 4 is not odd.*
> *Therefore, the number 4 is even.*

Weak disjunct (both can be true):
> *Either Socrates is walking or talking.*
> *Socrates is not walking.*
> *Therefore he is talking.*

✳ **Conjunctive Syllogisms** - the first proposition contains two contradictories:

> *No whole number can be both odd and even.*
> *This whole number is not even.*
> *Therefore, this whole number is odd.*

✳ <u>The Dilemma</u>:

Has two "horns" either pointing to one conclusion or to two impossibilities.

> *Either A or B.*
> *If A then C.*
> *If B then C.*
> *Therefore, C.*

or:

> *Either A or B.*
> *If A then C.*
> *If B then D.*
> *Therefore either C or D.*

Ways out of a Dilemma:

1. Escaping between the horns - discovering a third possibility.
2. Taking the dilemma by the horns - denying one of the possibilities.
3. Rebutting a dilemma - comes up with a counter dilemma.

<u>Expository Syllogisms</u> - have a singular middle term:

> *Socrates was a philosopher.*
> *Socraes was a Greek.*
> *Therefore, a Greek was a philosopher.*

Not really a syllogism, or useful in any way.

NON-CATEGORICAL SYLLOGISMS – SUPPLEMENT

1 Corinthians 15:12-32:

Now if Christ is preached as raised from the dead, how can some of you say that there is no resurrection of the dead? But if there is no resurrection of the dead, then Christ has not been raised; if Christ has not been raised, then our preaching is in vain and your faith is in vain. We are even found to be misrepresenting God, because we testified of God that he raised Christ, whom he did not raise if it is true that the dead are not raised. For if the dead are not raised, then Christ has not been raised. If Christ has not been raised, your faith is futile and you are still in your sins. Then those also who have fallen asleep in Christ have perished. If for this life only we have hoped in Christ, we are of all men most to be pitied. But in fact Christ has been raised from the dead, the first fruits of those who have fallen asleep. For as by a man came death, by a man has come also the resurrection of the dead. For as in Adam all die, so also in Christ shall all be made alive. But each in his own order: Christ the first fruits, then at his coming those who belong to Christ. Then comes the end, when he delivers the kingdom to God the Father after destroying every rule and every authority and power. For he must reign until he has put all his enemies under his feet. The last enemy to be destroyed is death. "For God has put all things in subjection under his feet." But when it says, "All things are put in subjection under him," it is plain that he is excepted who put all things under him. When all things are subjected to him, then the Son himself will also be subjected to him who put all things under him, that God may be everything to every one. Otherwise, what do people mean by being baptized on behalf of the dead? If the dead are not raised at all, why are people baptized on their behalf? Why am I in peril every hour? I protest, brethren, by my pride in you which I have in Christ Jesus our Lord, I die every day! What do I gain if, humanly speaking, I fought with beasts at Ephesus? If the dead are not raised, "Let us eat and drink, for tomorrow we die."

From St. Thomas Aquinas, *Summa Contra Gentiles* I.15.6:

The force of Aristotle's argument lies in this: if something moves itself primarily and through itself, rather than through its parts, then insofar as it is moved it cannot depend on another. But the moving of the divisible itself, like its being, depends on its parts; it cannot therefore move itself primarily and through itself. Hence, for the truth of the inferred conclusion it is not necessary to assume as an absolute truth that a part of a being moving itself is at rest. What must rather be true is this conditional proposition: if the part were at rest, the whole would be at rest. Now, this proposition would be true even though its antecedent be impossible.

Matthew 6:22-34:

"The eye is the lamp of the body. So, if your eye is sound, your whole body will be full of light; but if your eye is not sound, your whole body will be full of darkness. If then the light in you is darkness, how great is the darkness!
"No one can serve two masters; for either he will hate the one and love the other, or he will be devoted to the one and despise the other. You cannot serve God and mammon.

"Therefore I tell you, do not be anxious about your life, what you shall eat or what you shall drink, nor about your body, what you shall put on. Is not life more than food, and the body more than clothing? Look at the birds of the air: they neither sow nor reap nor gather into barns, and yet your heavenly Father feeds them. Are you not of more value than they? And which of you by being anxious can add one cubit to his span of life? And why are you anxious about clothing? Consider the lilies of the field, how they grow; they neither toil nor spin; yet I tell you, even Solomon in all his glory was not arrayed like one of these. But if God so clothes the grass of the field, which today is alive and tomorrow is thrown into the oven, will he not much more clothe you, O men of little faith? Therefore do not be anxious, saying, `What shall we eat?' or `What shall we drink?' or `What shall we wear?' For the Gentiles seek all these things; and your heavenly Father knows that you need them all. But seek first his kingdom and his righteousness, and all these things shall be yours as well.

"Therefore do not be anxious about tomorrow, for tomorrow will be anxious for itself. Let the day's own trouble be sufficient for the day.

Sample Enthymemes

1. God does not exist because you can't find him in a test tube.

2. No one can move mountains, because mountains have no wheels.

3. Logic is boring because it's not musical.

4. I'm worth something because God loves me.

5. God loves me because I'm worth something.

6. Not all rich people are happy; some commit suicide.

7. I hate your dog because he barks at night.

8. Fred smells because he just worked out.

9. Oranges are delicious because they are citrus.

10. Guns and Roses is the greatest band ever because of Slash.

INDUCTION & OTHER STUFF

Aristotle, *Posterior Analytics,* tr. G. R. G. Mure, selections

Book I

Part 1

All instruction given or received by way of argument proceeds from pre-existent knowledge. This becomes evident upon a survey of all the species of such instruction. The mathematical sciences and all other speculative disciplines are acquired in this way, and so are the two forms of dialectical reasoning, syllogistic and inductive; for each of these latter make use of old knowledge to impart new, the syllogism assuming an audience that accepts its premisses, induction exhibiting the universal as implicit in the clearly known particular. Again, the persuasion exerted by rhetorical arguments is in principle the same, since they use either example, a kind of induction, or enthymeme, a form of syllogism.

The pre-existent knowledge required is of two kinds. In some cases admission of the fact must be assumed, in others comprehension of the meaning of the term used, and sometimes both assumptions are essential. Thus, we assume that every predicate can be either truly affirmed or truly denied of any subject, and that 'triangle' means so and so; as regards 'unit' we have to make the double assumption of the meaning of the word and the existence of the thing. The reason is that these several objects are not equally obvious to us. Recognition of a truth may in some cases contain as factors both previous knowledge and also knowledge acquired simultaneously with that recognition-knowledge, this latter, of the particulars actually falling under the universal and therein already virtually known. For example, the student knew beforehand that the angles of every triangle are equal to two right angles; but it was only at the actual moment at which he was being led on to recognize this as true in the instance before him that he came to know 'this figure inscribed in the semicircle' to be a triangle. For some things (viz. the singulars finally reached which are not predicable of anything else as subject) are only learnt in this way, i.e. there is here no recognition through a middle of a minor term as subject to a major. Before he was led on to recognition or before he actually drew a conclusion, we should perhaps say that in a manner he knew, in a manner not.

If he did not in an unqualified sense of the term know the existence of this triangle, how could he know without qualification that its angles were equal to two right angles? No: clearly he knows not without qualification but only in the sense that he knows universally. If this distinction is not drawn, we are faced with the dilemma in the Meno: either a man will learn nothing or what he already knows; for we cannot accept the solution which some people offer. A man is asked, 'Do you, or do you not, know that every pair is even?' He says he does know it. The questioner then produces a particular pair, of the existence, and so a fortiori of the evenness, of which he was unaware. The solution which some people offer is to assert that they do not know that every pair is even, but only that everything which they know to be a pair is even: yet what they know to be even is that of which they have demonstrated evenness, i.e. what they made the subject of their premiss, viz. not merely every triangle or number which they know to be such, but any and every number or triangle without reservation. For no premiss is ever couched in the form 'every number which you know to be such', or 'every rectilinear figure which you know to be such': the predicate is always construed as applicable to any and every instance of the thing. On the other hand, I imagine there is nothing to prevent a man in one sense knowing what he is learning, in another not knowing it. The strange thing would be, not if in some sense he knew what he was learning, but if he were to know it in that precise sense and manner in which he was learning it.

Part 2

We suppose ourselves to possess unqualified scientific knowledge of a thing, as opposed to knowing it in the accidental way in which the sophist knows, when we think that we know the cause on which the fact depends, as the cause of that fact and of no other, and, further, that the fact could not be other than it is. Now that scientific knowing is something of this sort is evident-witness both those who falsely claim it and those who actually possess it, since the former merely imagine themselves to be, while the latter are also actually, in the condition described. Consequently the proper object of unqualified scientific knowledge is something which cannot be other than it is.

There may be another manner of knowing as well-that will be discussed later. What I now assert is that at all events we do know by demonstration. By demonstration I mean a syllogism productive of scientific knowledge, a syllogism, that is, the grasp of which is eo ipso such knowledge. Assuming then that my thesis as to the nature of scientific knowing is correct, the premisses of demonstrated knowledge must be true, primary, immediate, better known than and prior to the conclusion, which is further related to them as effect to cause. Unless these conditions are satisfied, the basic truths will not be 'appropriate' to the conclusion. Syllogism there may indeed be without these conditions, but such syllogism, not being productive of scientific knowledge, will not be demonstration. The premisses must be true: for that which is non-existent cannot be known-we cannot know, e.g. that the diagonal of a square is commensurate with its side. The premisses must be primary and indemonstrable; otherwise they will require demonstration in order to be known, since to have knowledge, if it be not accidental knowledge, of things which are demonstrable, means precisely to have a demonstration of them. The premisses must be the causes of the conclusion, better known than it, and prior to it; its causes, since we possess scientific knowledge of a thing only when we know its cause; prior, in order to be causes; antecedently known, this antecedent knowledge being not our mere understanding of the meaning, but knowledge of the fact as well. Now 'prior' and 'better known' are ambiguous terms, for there is a difference between what is prior and better known in the order of being and what is prior and better known to man. I mean that objects nearer to sense are prior and better known to man; objects without qualification prior and better known are those further from sense. Now the most universal causes are furthest from sense and particular causes are nearest to sense, and they are thus exactly opposed to one another. In saying that the premisses of demonstrated knowledge must be primary, I mean that they must be the 'appropriate' basic truths, for I identify primary premiss and basic truth. A 'basic truth' in a demonstration is an immediate proposition. An immediate proposition is one which has no other proposition prior to it. A proposition is either part of an enunciation, i.e. it predicates a single attribute of a single subject. If a proposition is dialectical, it assumes either part indifferently; if it is demonstrative, it lays down one part to the definite exclusion of the other because that part is true. The term 'enunciation' denotes either part of a contradiction indifferently. A contradiction is an opposition which of its own nature excludes a middle. The part of a contradiction which conjoins a predicate with a subject is an affirmation; the part disjoining them is a negation. I call an immediate basic truth of syllogism a 'thesis' when, though it is not susceptible of proof by the teacher, yet ignorance of it does not constitute a total bar to progress on the part of the pupil: one which the pupil must know if he is to learn anything whatever is an axiom. I call it an axiom because there are such truths and we give them the name of axioms par excellence. If a thesis assumes one part or the other of an enunciation, i.e. asserts either the existence or the non-existence of a subject, it is a hypothesis; if it does not so assert, it is a definition. Definition is a 'thesis' or a 'laying something down', since the arithmetician lays it down that to be a unit is to be quantitatively indivisible; but it is not a hypothesis, for to define what a unit is is not the same as to affirm its existence.

Now since the required ground of our knowledge-i.e. of our conviction-of a fact is the possession of such a syllogism as we call demonstration, and the ground of the syllogism is the facts constituting its premisses, we must not only know the primary premisses-some if not all of them-beforehand, but know them better than the conclusion: for the cause of an attribute's inherence in a subject always itself inheres in the subject more firmly than that attribute; e.g. the cause of our loving anything is dearer to us than the object of our love. So since the primary premisses are the cause of our knowledge-i.e. of our conviction-it follows that we know them better-that is, are more convinced of them-than their consequences, precisely because of our knowledge of the latter is the effect of our knowledge of the premisses. Now a man cannot believe in anything more than in the things he knows, unless he has either actual knowledge of it or something better than actual knowledge. But we are faced with this paradox if a student whose belief rests on demonstration has not prior knowledge; a man must believe in some, if not in all, of the basic truths more than in the conclusion. Moreover, if a man sets out to acquire the scientific knowledge that comes through demonstration, he must not only have a better knowledge of the basic truths and a firmer conviction of them than of the connexion which is being demonstrated: more than this, nothing must be more certain or better known to him than these basic truths in their character as contradicting the fundamental premisses which lead to the opposed and erroneous conclusion. For indeed the conviction of pure science must be unshakable.

Part 3

Some hold that, owing to the necessity of knowing the primary premisses, there is no scientific knowledge. Others think there is, but that all truths are demonstrable. Neither doctrine is either true or a necessary deduction from the premisses. The first school, assuming that there is no way of knowing other than by demonstration, maintain that an infinite regress is involved, on the ground that if behind the prior stands no primary, we could not know the posterior through the prior (wherein they are right, for one cannot traverse an infinite series): if on the other hand-they say-the series terminates and there are primary premisses, yet these are unknowable because incapable of demonstration, which according to them is the only form of knowledge. And since thus one cannot know the primary premisses, knowledge of the conclusions which follow from them is not pure scientific knowledge nor properly knowing at all, but rests on the mere supposition that the premisses are true. The other party agree with them as regards knowing, holding that it is only possible by demonstration, but they see no difficulty in holding that all truths are demonstrated, on the ground that demonstration may be circular and reciprocal.

Our own doctrine is that not all knowledge is demonstrative: on the contrary, knowledge of the immediate premisses is independent of demonstration. (The necessity of this is obvious; for since we must know the prior premisses from which the demonstration is drawn, and since the regress must end in immediate truths, those truths must be indemonstrable.) Such, then, is our doctrine, and in addition we maintain that besides scientific knowledge there is its originative source which enables us to recognize the definitions.

Now demonstration must be based on premises prior to and better known than the conclusion; and the same things cannot simultaneously be both prior and posterior to one another: so circular demonstration is clearly not possible in the unqualified sense of 'demonstration', but only possible if 'demonstration' be extended to include that other method of argument which rests on a distinction between truths prior to us and truths without qualification prior, i.e. the method by which induction produces knowledge. But if we accept this extension of its meaning, our definition of unqualified knowledge will prove faulty; for there seem to be two kinds of it. Perhaps, however, the second form of demonstration, that which proceeds from truths better known to us, is not demonstration in the unqualified sense of the term.

The advocates of circular demonstration are not only faced with the difficulty we have just stated: in addition their theory reduces to the mere statement that if a thing exists, then it does exist-an easy way of proving anything. That this is so can be clearly shown by taking three terms, for to constitute the circle it makes no difference whether many terms or few or even only two are taken. Thus by direct proof, if A is, B must be; if B is, C must be; therefore if A is, C must be. Since then-by the circular proof-if A is, B must be, and if B is, A must be, A may be substituted for C above. Then 'if B is, A must be'='if B is, C must be', which above gave the conclusion 'if A is, C must be': but C and A have been identified. Consequently the upholders of circular demonstration are in the position of saying that if A is, A must be-a simple way of proving anything. Moreover, even such circular demonstration is impossible except in the case of attributes that imply one another, viz. 'peculiar' properties.

Now, it has been shown that the positing of one thing-be it one term or one premiss-never involves a necessary consequent: two premisses constitute the first and smallest foundation for drawing a conclusion at all and therefore a fortiori for the demonstrative syllogism of science. If, then, A is implied in B and C, and B and C are reciprocally implied in one another and in A, it is possible, as has been shown in my writings on the syllogism, to prove all the assumptions on which the original conclusion rested, by circular demonstration in the first figure. But it has also been shown that in the other figures either no conclusion is possible, or at least none which proves both the original premisses. Propositions the terms of which are not convertible cannot be circularly demonstrated at all, and since convertible terms occur rarely in actual demonstrations, it is clearly frivolous and impossible to say that demonstration is reciprocal and that therefore everything can be demonstrated.

Part 4

Since the object of pure scientific knowledge cannot be other than it is, the truth obtained by demonstrative knowledge will be necessary. And since demonstrative knowledge is only present when we have a demonstration, it follows that demonstration is an inference from necessary premisses. So we must consider what are the premisses of demonstration-i.e. what is their character: and as a preliminary, let us define what we mean by an attribute 'true in every instance of its subject', an 'essential' attribute, and a 'commensurate and universal' attribute. I call 'true in every instance' what is truly predicable of all instances-not of one to the exclusion of others-and at all times, not at this or that time only; e.g. if animal is truly predicable of every instance of man, then if it be true to say 'this is a man', 'this is an animal' is also true, and if the one be true now the other is true now. A corresponding account holds if point is in every instance predicable as contained in line. There is evidence for this in the fact that the objection we raise against a proposition put to us as true in every instance is either an instance in which, or an occasion on which, it is not true. Essential attributes are (1) such as belong to their subject as elements in its essential nature (e.g. line thus belongs to triangle, point to line; for the very being or 'substance' of triangle and line is composed of these elements, which are contained in the formulae defining triangle and line): (2) such that, while they belong to certain subjects, the subjects to which they belong are contained in the attribute's own defining formula. Thus straight and curved belong to line, odd and even, prime and compound, square and oblong, to number; and also the formula defining any one of these attributes contains its subject-e.g. line or number as the case may be.

Extending this classification to all other attributes, I distinguish those that answer the above description as belonging essentially to their respective subjects; whereas attributes related in neither of these two ways to their subjects I call accidents or 'coincidents'; e.g. musical or white is a 'coincident' of animal.

Further (a) that is essential which is not predicated of a subject other than itself: e.g. 'the walking [thing]' walks and is white in virtue of being something else besides; whereas substance, in the sense of whatever signifies a 'this somewhat', is not what it is in virtue of being something else besides. Things, then, not predicated of a subject I call essential; things predicated of a subject I call accidental or 'coincidental'.

In another sense again (b) a thing consequentially connected with anything is essential; one not so connected is 'coincidental'. An example of the latter is 'While he was walking it lightened': the lightning was not due to his walking; it was, we should say, a coincidence. If, on the other hand, there is a consequential connexion, the predication is essential; e.g. if a beast dies when its throat is being cut, then its death is also essentially connected with the cutting, because the cutting was the cause of death, not death a 'coincident' of the cutting.

So far then as concerns the sphere of connexions scientifically known in the unqualified sense of that term, all attributes which (within that sphere) are essential either in the sense that their subjects are contained in them, or in the sense that they are contained in their subjects, are necessary as well as consequentially connected with their subjects. For it is impossible for them not to inhere in their subjects either simply or in the qualified sense that one or other of a pair of opposites must inhere in the subject; e.g. in line must be either straightness or curvature, in number either oddness or evenness. For within a single identical genus the contrary of a given attribute is either its privative or its contradictory; e.g. within number what is not odd is even, inasmuch as within this sphere even is a necessary consequent of not-odd. So, since any given predicate must be either affirmed or denied of any subject, essential attributes must inhere in their subjects of necessity.

Thus, then, we have established the distinction between the attribute which is 'true in every instance' and the 'essential' attribute.

I term 'commensurately universal' an attribute which belongs to every instance of its subject, and to every instance essentially and as such; from which it clearly follows that all commensurate universals inhere necessarily in their subjects. The essential attribute, and the attribute that belongs to its subject as such, are identical. E.g. point and straight belong to line essentially, for they belong to line as such; and triangle as such has two right angles, for it is essentially equal to two right angles.

An attribute belongs commensurately and universally to a subject when it can be shown to belong to any random instance of that subject and when the subject is the first thing to which it can be shown to belong. Thus, e.g. (1) the equality of its angles to two right angles is not a commensurately universal attribute of figure. For though it is possible to show that a figure has its angles equal to two right angles, this attribute cannot be demonstrated of any figure selected at haphazard, nor in demonstrating does one take a figure at random-a square is a figure but its angles are not equal to two right angles. On the other hand, any isosceles triangle has its angles equal to two right angles, yet isosceles triangle is not the primary subject of this attribute but triangle is prior. So whatever can be shown to have its angles equal to two right angles, or to possess any other attribute, in any random instance of itself and primarily-that is the first subject to which the predicate in question belongs commensurately and universally, and the demonstration, in the essential sense, of any predicate is the proof of it as belonging to this first subject commensurately and universally: while the proof of it as belonging to the other subjects to which it attaches is demonstration only in a secondary and unessential sense. Nor again (2) is equality to two right angles a commensurately universal attribute of isosceles; it is of wider application.

...

Part 31

Scientific knowledge is not possible through the act of perception. Even if perception as a faculty is of 'the such' and not merely of a 'this somewhat', yet one must at any rate actually perceive a 'this somewhat', and at a definite present place and time: but that which is commensurately universal and true in all cases one cannot perceive, since it is not 'this' and it is not 'now'; if it were, it would not be commensurately universal-the term we apply to what is always and everywhere. Seeing, therefore, that demonstrations are commensurately universal and universals imperceptible, we clearly cannot obtain scientific knowledge by the act of perception: nay, it is obvious that even if it were possible to perceive that a triangle has its angles equal to two right angles, we should still be looking for a demonstration-we should not (as some say) possess knowledge of it; for perception must be of a particular, whereas scientific knowledge involves the recognition of the commensurate universal. So if we were on the moon, and saw the earth shutting out the sun's light, we should not know the cause of the eclipse: we should perceive the present fact of the eclipse, but not the reasoned fact at all, since the act of perception is not of the commensurate universal. I do not, of course, deny that by watching the frequent recurrence of this event we might, after tracking the commensurate universal, possess a demonstration, for the commensurate universal is elicited from the several groups of singulars.

The commensurate universal is precious because it makes clear the cause; so that in the case of facts like these which have a cause other than themselves universal knowledge is more precious than sense-perceptions and than intuition. (As regards primary truths there is of course a different account to be given.) Hence it is clear that knowledge of things demonstrable cannot be acquired by perception, unless the term perception is applied to the possession of scientific knowledge through demonstration. Nevertheless certain points do arise with regard to connexions to be proved which are referred for their explanation to a failure in sense-perception: there are cases when an act of vision would terminate our inquiry, not because in seeing we should be knowing, but because we should have elicited the universal from seeing; if, for example, we saw the pores in the glass and the light passing through, the reason of the kindling would be clear to us because we should at the same time see it in each instance and intuit that it must be so in all instances.

...

Book II

Part 1

The kinds of question we ask are as many as the kinds of things which we know. They are in fact four:-(1) whether the connexion of an attribute with a thing is a fact, (2) what is the reason of the connexion, (3) whether a thing exists, (4) What is the nature of the thing. Thus, when our question concerns a complex of thing and attribute and we ask whether the thing is thus or otherwise qualified-whether, e.g. the sun suffers eclipse or not-then we are asking as to the fact of a connexion. That our inquiry ceases with the discovery that the sun does suffer eclipse is an indication of this; and if we know from the start that the sun suffers eclipse, we do not inquire whether it does so or not. On the other hand, when we know the fact we ask the reason; as, for example, when we know that the sun is being eclipsed and that an earthquake is in progress, it is the reason of eclipse or earthquake into which we inquire.

Where a complex is concerned, then, those are the two questions we ask; but for some objects of inquiry we have a different kind of question to ask, such as whether there is or is not a centaur or a God. (By 'is or is not' I mean 'is or is not, without further qualification'; as opposed to 'is or is not [e.g.] white'.) On the other hand, when we have ascertained the thing's existence, we inquire as to its nature, asking, for instance, 'what, then, is God?' or 'what is man?'.

Part 2

These, then, are the four kinds of question we ask, and it is in the answers to these questions that our knowledge consists.

Now when we ask whether a connexion is a fact, or whether a thing without qualification is, we are really asking whether the connexion or the thing has a 'middle'; and when we have ascertained either that the connexion is a fact or that the thing is-i.e. ascertained either the partial or the unqualified being of the thing-and are proceeding to ask the reason of the connexion or the nature of the thing, then we are asking what the 'middle' is.

(By distinguishing the fact of the connexion and the existence of the thing as respectively the partial and the unqualified being of the thing, I mean that if we ask 'does the moon suffer eclipse?', or 'does the moon wax?', the question concerns a part of the thing's being; for what we are asking in such questions is whether a thing is this or that, i.e. has or has not this or that attribute: whereas, if we ask whether the moon or night exists, the question concerns the unqualified being of a thing.)

We conclude that in all our inquiries we are asking either whether there is a 'middle' or what the 'middle' is: for the 'middle' here is precisely the cause, and it is the cause that we seek in all our inquiries. Thus, 'Does the moon suffer eclipse?' means 'Is there or is there not a cause producing eclipse of the moon?', and when we have learnt that there is, our next question is, 'What, then, is this cause? for the cause through which a thing is-not is this or that, i.e. has this or that attribute, but without qualification is-and the cause through which it is-not is without qualification, but is this or that as having some essential attribute or some accident-are both alike the middle'. By that which is without qualification I mean the subject, e.g. moon or earth or sun or triangle; by that which a subject is (in the partial sense) I mean a property, e.g. eclipse, equality or inequality, interposition or non-interposition. For in all these examples it is clear that the nature of the thing and the reason of the fact are identical: the question 'What is eclipse?' and its answer 'The privation of the moon's light by the interposition of the earth' are identical with the question 'What is the reason of eclipse?' or 'Why does the moon suffer eclipse?' and the reply 'Because of the failure of light through the earth's shutting it out'. Again, for 'What is a concord? A commensurate numerical ratio of a high and a low note', we may substitute 'What ratio makes a high and a low note concordant? Their relation according to a commensurate numerical ratio.' 'Are the high and the low note concordant?' is equivalent to 'Is their ratio commensurate?'; and when we find that it is commensurate, we ask 'What, then, is their ratio?'.

Cases in which the 'middle' is sensible show that the object of our inquiry is always the 'middle': we inquire, because we have not perceived it, whether there is or is not a 'middle' causing, e.g. an eclipse. On the other hand, if we were on the moon we should not be inquiring either as to the fact or the reason, but both fact and reason would be obvious simultaneously. For the act of perception would have enabled us to know the universal too; since, the present fact of an eclipse being evident, perception would then at the same time give us the present fact of the earth's screening the sun's light, and from this would arise the universal.

Thus, as we maintain, to know a thing's nature is to know the reason why it is; and this is equally true of things in so far as they are said without qualification to he as opposed to being possessed of some attribute, and in so far as they are said to be possessed of some attribute such as equal to right angles, or greater or less.

Part 3

It is clear, then, that all questions are a search for a 'middle'. Let us now state how essential nature is revealed and in what way it can be reduced to demonstration; what definition is, and what things are definable. And let us first discuss certain difficulties which these questions raise, beginning what we have to say with a point most intimately connected with our immediately preceding remarks, namely the doubt that might be felt as to whether or not it is possible to know the same thing in the same relation, both by definition and by demonstration. It might, I mean, be urged that definition is held to concern essential nature and is in every case universal and affirmative; whereas, on the other hand, some conclusions are negative and some are not universal; e.g. all in the second figure are negative, none in the third are universal. And again, not even all affirmative conclusions in the first figure are definable, e.g. 'every triangle has its angles equal to two right angles'. An argument proving this difference between demonstration and definition is that to have scientific knowledge of the demonstrable is identical with possessing a demonstration of it: hence if demonstration of such conclusions as these is possible, there clearly cannot also be definition of them. If there could, one might know such a conclusion also in virtue of its definition without possessing the demonstration of it; for there is nothing to stop our having the one without the other.

Induction too will sufficiently convince us of this difference; for never yet by defining anything-essential attribute or accident-did we get knowledge of it. Again, if to define is to acquire knowledge of a substance, at any rate such attributes are not substances.

It is evident, then, that not everything demonstrable can be defined. What then? Can everything definable be demonstrated, or not? There is one of our previous arguments which covers this too. Of a single thing qua single there is a single scientific knowledge. Hence, since to know the demonstrable scientifically is to possess the demonstration of it, an impossible consequence will follow:-possession of its definition without its demonstration will give knowledge of the demonstrable.

Moreover, the basic premisses of demonstrations are definitions, and it has already been shown that these will be found indemonstrable; either the basic premisses will be demonstrable and will depend on prior premisses, and the regress will be endless; or the primary truths will be indemonstrable definitions.

But if the definable and the demonstrable are not wholly the same, may they yet be partially the same? Or is that impossible, because there can be no demonstration of the definable? There can be none, because definition is of the essential nature or being of something, and all demonstrations evidently posit and assume the essential nature-mathematical demonstrations, for example, the nature of unity and the odd, and all the other sciences likewise. Moreover, every demonstration proves a predicate of a subject as attaching or as not attaching to it, but in definition one thing is not predicated of another; we do not, e.g. predicate animal of biped nor biped of animal, nor yet figure of plane-plane not being figure nor figure plane. Again, to prove essential nature is not the same as to prove the fact of a connexion. Now definition reveals essential nature, demonstration reveals that a given attribute attaches or does not attach to a given subject; but different things require different demonstrations-unless the one demonstration is related to the other as part to whole. I add this because if all triangles have been proved to possess angles equal to two right angles, then this attribute has been proved to attach to isosceles; for isosceles is a part of which all triangles constitute the whole. But in the case before us the fact and the essential nature are not so related to one another, since the one is not a part of the other.

So it emerges that not all the definable is demonstrable nor all the demonstrable definable; and we may draw the general conclusion that there is no identical object of which it is possible to possess both a definition and a demonstration. It follows obviously that definition and demonstration are neither identical nor contained either within the other: if they were, their objects would be related either as identical or as whole and part.

Part 4

So much, then, for the first stage of our problem. The next step is to raise the question whether syllogism-i.e. demonstration-of the definable nature is possible or, as our recent argument assumed, impossible.

We might argue it impossible on the following grounds:-(a) syllogism proves an attribute of a subject through the middle term; on the other hand (b) its definable nature is both 'peculiar' to a subject and predicated of it as belonging to its essence. But in that case (1) the subject, its definition, and the middle term connecting them must be reciprocally predicable of one another; for if A is to C, obviously A is 'peculiar' to B and B to C-in fact all three terms are 'peculiar' to one another: and further (2) if A inheres in the essence of all B and B is predicated universally of all C as belonging to C's essence, A also must be predicated of C as belonging to its essence.

If one does not take this relation as thus duplicated-if, that is, A is predicated as being of the essence of B, but B is not of the essence of the subjects of which it is predicated-A will not necessarily be predicated of C as belonging to its essence. So both premisses will predicate essence, and consequently B also will be predicated of C as its essence. Since, therefore, both premisses do predicate essence-i.e. definable form-C's definable form will appear in the middle term before the conclusion is drawn.

We may generalize by supposing that it is possible to prove the essential nature of man. Let C be man, A man's essential nature--two-footed animal, or aught else it may be. Then, if we are to syllogize, A must be predicated of all B. But this premiss will be mediated by a fresh definition, which consequently will also be the essential nature of man. Therefore the argument assumes what it has to prove, since B too is the essential nature of man. It is, however, the case in which there are only the two premisses-i.e. in which the premisses are primary and immediate-which we ought to investigate, because it best illustrates the point under discussion.

Thus they who prove the essential nature of soul or man or anything else through reciprocating terms beg the question. It would be begging the question, for example, to contend that the soul is that which causes its own life, and that what causes its own life is a self-moving number; for one would have to postulate that the soul is a self-moving number in the sense of being identical with it. For if A is predicable as a mere consequent of B and B of C, A will not on that account be the definable form of C: A will merely be what it was true to say of C. Even if A is predicated of all B inasmuch as B is identical with a species of A, still it will not follow: being an animal is predicated of being a man-since it is true that in all instances to be human is to be animal, just as it is also true that every man is an animal-but not as identical with being man.

We conclude, then, that unless one takes both the premisses as predicating essence, one cannot infer that A is the definable form and essence of C: but if one does so take them, in assuming B one will have assumed, before drawing the conclusion, what the definable form of C is; so that there has been no inference, for one has begged the question.

...

Part 11

We think we have scientific knowledge when we know the cause, and there are four causes: (1) the definable form, (2) an antecedent which necessitates a consequent, (3) the efficient cause, (4) the final cause. Hence each of these can be the middle term of a proof, for (a) though the inference from antecedent to necessary consequent does not hold if only one premiss is assumed-two is the minimum-still when there are two it holds on condition that they have a single common middle term. So it is from the assumption of this single middle term that the conclusion follows necessarily. The following example will also show this. Why is the angle in a semicircle a right angle?-or from what assumption does it follow that it is a right angle? Thus, let A be right angle, B the half of two right angles, C the angle in a semicircle. Then B is the cause in virtue of which A, right angle, is attributable to C, the angle in a semicircle, since B=A and the

248

other, viz. C,=B, for C is half of two right angles. Therefore it is the assumption of B, the half of two right angles, from which it follows that A is attributable to C, i.e. that the angle in a semicircle is a right angle. Moreover, B is identical with (b) the defining form of A, since it is what A's definition signifies. Moreover, the formal cause has already been shown to be the middle. (c) 'Why did the Athenians become involved in the Persian war?' means 'What cause originated the waging of war against the Athenians?' and the answer is, 'Because they raided Sardis with the Eretrians', since this originated the war. Let A be war, B unprovoked raiding, C the Athenians. Then B, unprovoked raiding, is true of C, the Athenians, and A is true of B, since men make war on the unjust aggressor. So A, having war waged upon them, is true of B, the initial aggressors, and B is true of C, the Athenians, who were the aggressors. Hence here too the cause-in this case the efficient cause-is the middle term. (d) This is no less true where the cause is the final cause. E.g. why does one take a walk after supper? For the sake of one's health. Why does a house exist? For the preservation of one's goods. The end in view is in the one case health, in the other preservation. To ask the reason why one must walk after supper is precisely to ask to what end one must do it. Let C be walking after supper, B the non-regurgitation of food, A health. Then let walking after supper possess the property of preventing food from rising to the orifice of the stomach, and let this condition be healthy; since it seems that B, the non-regurgitation of food, is attributable to C, taking a walk, and that A, health, is attributable to B. What, then, is the cause through which A, the final cause, inheres in C? It is B, the non-regurgitation of food; but B is a kind of definition of A, for A will be explained by it. Why is B the cause of A's belonging to C? Because to be in a condition such as B is to be in health. The definitions must be transposed, and then the detail will become clearer. Incidentally, here the order of coming to be is the reverse of what it is in proof through the efficient cause: in the efficient order the middle term must come to be first, whereas in the teleological order the minor, C, must first take place, and the end in view comes last in time.

The same thing may exist for an end and be necessitated as well. For example, light shines through a lantern (1) because that which consists of relatively small particles necessarily passes through pores larger than those particles-assuming that light does issue by penetration- and (2) for an end, namely to save us from stumbling. If then, a thing can exist through two causes, can it come to be through two causes-as for instance if thunder be a hiss and a roar necessarily produced by the quenching of fire, and also designed, as the Pythagoreans say, for a threat to terrify those that lie in Tartarus? Indeed, there are very many such cases, mostly among the processes and products of the natural world; for nature, in different senses of the term 'nature', produces now for an end, now by necessity.

Necessity too is of two kinds. It may work in accordance with a thing's natural tendency, or by constraint and in opposition to it; as, for instance, by necessity a stone is borne both upwards and downwards, but not by the same necessity.

Of the products of man's intelligence some are never due to chance or necessity but always to an end, as for example a house or a statue; others, such as health or safety, may result from chance as well.

It is mostly in cases where the issue is indeterminate (though only where the production does not originate in chance, and the end is consequently good), that a result is due to an end, and this is true alike in nature or in art. By chance, on the other hand, nothing comes to be for an end.

Part 19

As regards syllogism and demonstration, the definition of, and the conditions required to produce each of them, are now clear, and with that also the definition of, and the conditions required to produce, demonstrative knowledge, since it is the same as demonstration. As to the basic premisses, how they become known and what is the developed state of knowledge of them is made clear by raising some preliminary problems.

We have already said that scientific knowledge through demonstration is impossible unless a man knows the primary immediate premisses. But there are questions which might be raised in respect of the apprehension of these immediate premisses: one might not only ask whether it is of the same kind as the apprehension of the conclusions, but also whether there is or is not scientific knowledge of both; or scientific knowledge of the latter, and of the former a different kind of knowledge; and, further, whether the developed states of knowledge are not innate but come to be in us, or are innate but at first unnoticed. Now it is strange if we possess them from birth; for it means that we possess apprehensions more accurate than demonstration and fail to notice them. If on the other hand we acquire them and do not previously possess them, how could we apprehend and learn without a basis of pre-existent knowledge? For that is impossible, as we used to find in the case of demonstration. So it emerges that neither can we possess them from birth, nor can they come to be in us if we are without knowledge of them to the extent of having no such developed state at all. Therefore we must possess a capacity of some sort, but not such as to rank higher in accuracy than these developed states. And this at least is an obvious characteristic of all animals, for they possess a congenital discriminative capacity which is called sense-perception. But though sense-perception is innate in all animals, in some the sense-impression comes to persist, in others it does not. So animals in which this persistence does not come to be have either no knowledge at all outside the act of perceiving, or no knowledge of objects of which no impression persists; animals in which it does come into being have perception and can continue to retain the sense-impression in the soul: and when such persistence is frequently repeated a further distinction at once arises between those which out of the persistence of such sense-impressions develop a power of systematizing them and those which do not. So out of sense-perception comes to be what we call memory, and out of frequently repeated memories of the same thing develops experience; for a number of memories constitute a single experience. From experience again-i.e. from the universal now stabilized in its entirety within the soul, the one beside the many which is a single identity within them all-originate the skill of the craftsman and the knowledge of the man of science, skill in the sphere of coming to be and science in the sphere of being.

We conclude that these states of knowledge are neither innate in a determinate form, nor developed from other higher states of knowledge, but from sense-perception. It is like a rout in battle stopped by first one man making a stand and then another, until the original formation has been restored. The soul is so constituted as to be capable of this process.

Let us now restate the account given already, though with insufficient clearness. When one of a number of logically indiscriminable particulars has made a stand, the earliest universal is present in the soul: for though the act of sense-perception is of the particular, its content is universal-is man, for example, not the man Callias. A fresh stand is made among these rudimentary universals, and the process does not cease until the indivisible concepts, the true universals, are established: e.g. such and such a species of animal is a step towards the genus animal, which by the same process is a step towards a further generalization.

Thus it is clear that we must get to know the primary premisses by induction; for the method by which even sense-perception implants the universal is inductive. Now of the thinking states by which we grasp truth, some are unfailingly true, others admit of error-opinion, for instance, and calculation, whereas scientific knowing and intuition are always true: further, no other kind of thought except intuition is more accurate than scientific knowledge, whereas primary premisses are more knowable than demonstrations, and all scientific knowledge is discursive. From these considerations it follows that there will be no scientific knowledge of the primary premisses, and since except intuition nothing can be truer than scientific knowledge, it will be intuition that apprehends the primary premisses-a result which also follows from the fact that demonstration cannot be the originative source of demonstration, nor, consequently, scientific knowledge of scientific knowledge.If, therefore, it is the only other kind of true thinking except scientific knowing, intuition will be the originative source of scientific knowledge. And the originative source of science grasps the original basic premiss, while science as a whole is similarly related as originative source to the whole body of fact.

Key for Symbolic Logic:

p, q, r, s, etc. = propositions (can be pos. or neg.)

~ = "not" (can be used with both pos. and neg. props.)

⊃ = "implies"

∴ = "therefore"

v = "or" (as in "Either…or")

& or • = "and"

≡ = "if and only if"

HYPOTHETICAL SYLLOGISMS
If [*antecedent*], then [*consequent*].

Pure Hypothetical Syllogisms:

If it rains, I will get wet.	p ⊃q
If it gets wet, I will be cold.	q ⊃r
Therefore, if it rains, I will be cold.	∴ p ⊃ r

Valid Conditional Syllogisms:

Affirming the Antecedent (AA):

If even Socrates lacks wisdom, no man is wise.	p ⊃q
Socrates lacks wisdom.	p
Therefore, no man is wise.	∴ q

Denying the Consequent (DC):

If there is food here, I will smell it.	p ⊃q
I don't smell it.	~q
Therefore, there is no food.	∴ ~p

Invalid Conditional Syllogisms:

Affirming the Consequent (AC):

If we are in a tornado, the house is falling apart.	p ⊃q
The house is falling apart.	q
Therefore, we are in a tornado.	∴ p

Denying the Antecedent (DA):

If we're lottery winners, we're rich.	p ⊃q
We're not lottery winners.	~p
Therefore, we're not rich.	∴ ~q

Disjunctive Syllogisms:

He is either a villain or a fool.	p v q
He's no fool.	~p
Therefore he's a villain.	∴ q

Conjunctive Syllogisms:

You cannot have your cake and eat it too.	~(p v q)
You ate your cake.	q
Therefore, you don't have it anymore.	∴ ~p

Reductio Ad Absurdum **Arguments**

Begin with the opponent's view and explore the consequences, reaching one that is absurd:

If there is no First Mover, then there are no intermediate movers. If there are no intermediate movers, there is no motion. ← *Resulting absurdity.*

INDUCTION

Induction seeks to arrive at **causes** through examining **effects.** There are different ways to describe causality:

<u>Natural vs. Logical Causality:</u>

Natural Causes cause the *thing*, whereas Logical Causality causes the *knowledge of the thing*.

Natural Cause - "How did he break the wall?" "He drove into it."
Logical Cause - "How do you know he broke the wall?" "He told me so."

<u>The Four Causes:</u>

Material – "It fell because its atoms are heavy."
Formal – "It fell because it is a bowling ball, and that's what bowling balls do."
Efficient – "It fell because I dropped it on your foot."
Final – "I dropped the bowling ball on your foot because I don't like your face."

Necessary vs. Sufficient Causality:

A Necessary Cause is *required* for the effect to occur; a Sufficient Cause is *enough alone* for the effect.

Necessary Cause – "You need to turn the key if your car is to start." (not to mention gas, oil, etc.)

Sufficient Cause – "All you need to make vinegar is some wine and some time."

Ultimate vs. Proximate Causes:

Ultimate Causes are "first" in causation (but not always in time); Proximate are "last," i.e., closer to the effect.

Ultimate/Remote/First Cause – "It was God's will that the bowling ball fell on your foot."

Proximate/Immediate/Second Cause – "It was my hand that dropped the bowling ball on your foot."

Scientific Method

MAKE AN OBSERVATION

ASK A QUESTION

FORM A HYPOTHESIS

CONDUCT AN EXPERIMENT

ACCEPT HYPOTHESIS

REJECT HYPOTHESIS

MILL'S METHODS TO DISCOVER CAUSALITY

1. Direct Method of Agreement

"If two or more instances of the phenomenon under investigation have only one circumstance in common, the circumstance in which alone all the instances agree, is the cause (or effect) of the given phenomenon."

All the people working at the power plant have cancer, and only they are, and the only difference between them and everyone else is the radiation they live with. The radiation must be causing the cancer.

2. Method of Difference

"If an instance in which the phenomenon under investigation occurs, and an instance in which it does not occur, have every circumstance in common save one, that one occurring only in the former; the circumstance in which alone the two instances differ, is the effect, or the cause, or an indispensable part of the cause, of the phenomenon."

The people working at the Springfield power plant are getting cancer, but not those in Shelbyville, but the only difference is that the Shelbyville plant workers eat White Castle. White Castle must prevent cancer.

3. Joint Method of Agreement and Difference

"If two or more instances in which the phenomenon occurs have only one circumstance in common, while two or more instances in which it does not occur have nothing in common save the absence of that circumstance: the circumstance in which alone the two sets of instances differ, is the effect, or cause, or a necessary part of the cause, of the phenomenon."

We then gave the Springfield plant workers White Castle, and they immediately stopped getting cancer.

4. Method of Residues
"Deduct from any phenomenon such part as is known by previous inductions to be the effect of certain antecedents, and the residue of the phenomenon is the effect of the remaining antecedents."

A balloon is heavier when it is full; air must therefore have weight.

5. Method of Concomitant Variations
"Whatever phenomenon varies in any manner whenever another phenomenon varies in some particular manner, is either a cause or an effect of that phenomenon, or is connected with it through some fact of causation."

Pipe smoking is linked to longer life since statistically pipe smokers live longer than non-smokers.

ARGUMENTS FROM ANALOGY

Work better as explanations or illustrations, since they do not actually prove anything, but making something clearer to the mind can aid an argument:

Every single person whose taste I admire really loved "Shutter Island," and every single person whose taste I abhor hated it. I would probably like it.

A Fortiori and *A Minore* Arguments

Arguments from Analogy that multiply the effect by making them "all the more" and "all the less."

A Fortiori – "If you, then, who are evil, know how to give good gifts to your children, how much more will your heavenly Father give good things to those who ask him."

A Minore – "I was able to run a marathon last week. I can totally make it up these stairs."

ESSAY STRUCTURE
(ONE OPTION)

Introduction
- Present the question
- Present the relevance of the question
- Present the possible debates/questions about it
- Present Thesis Statement*: a one-sentence summary of your paper.

Body
- Problem/question/point #1
    o Respond/answer/develop
- Problem/question/point #2
    o Respond/answer/develop
- Problem/question/point #3
    o Respond/answer/develop

Conclusion
- Reiterate thesis statement now that you've proven it
- Summarize points made in "Body" of the essay
- Never add new information in conclusion
- End creatively if you wish

*Thesis Statements are Syllogisms
- What is your conclusion?
    o This will show you your premises
- What are your premises?
    o These are your points to prove in the "Body"

SUMMA THEOLOGIAE I.2.1-3
ST. THOMAS AQUINAS

Article 1. Whether the existence of God is self-evident?

<u>Objection 1.</u> It seems that the existence of God is self-evident. Now those things are said to be self-evident to us the knowledge of which is naturally implanted in us, as we can see in regard to first principles. But as Damascene says (De Fide Orth. i, 1,3), "the knowledge of God is naturally implanted in all." Therefore the existence of God is self-evident.

<u>Objection 2.</u> Further, those things are said to be self-evident which are known as soon as the terms are known, which the Philosopher (1 Poster. iii) says is true of the first principles of demonstration. Thus, when the nature of a whole and of a part is known, it is at once recognized that every whole is greater than its part. But as soon as the signification of the word "God" is understood, it is at once seen that God exists. For by this word is signified that thing than which nothing greater can be conceived. But that which exists actually and mentally is greater than that which exists only mentally. Therefore, since as soon as the word "God" is understood it exists mentally, it also follows that it exists actually. Therefore the proposition "God exists" is self-evident.

<u>Objection 3.</u> Further, the existence of truth is self-evident. For whoever denies the existence of truth grants that truth does not exist: and, if truth does not exist, then the proposition "Truth does not exist" is true: and if there is anything true, there must be truth. But God is truth itself: "I

am the way, the truth, and the life" (John 14:6) Therefore "God exists" is self-evident.

On the contrary, No one can mentally admit the opposite of what is self-evident; as the Philosopher (Metaph. iv, lect. vi) states concerning the first principles of demonstration. But the opposite of the proposition "God is" can be mentally admitted: "The fool said in his heart, There is no God" (Psalm 52:1). Therefore, that God exists is not self-evident.

I answer that, A thing can be self-evident in either of two ways: on the one hand, self-evident in itself, though not to us; on the other, self-evident in itself, and to us. A proposition is self-evident because the predicate is included in the essence of the subject, as "Man is an animal," for animal is contained in the essence of man. If, therefore the essence of the predicate and subject be known to all, the proposition will be self-evident to all; as is clear with regard to the first principles of demonstration, the terms of which are common things that no one is ignorant of, such as being and non-being, whole and part, and such like. If, however, there are some to whom the essence of the predicate and subject is unknown, the proposition will be self-evident in itself, but not to those who do not know the meaning of the predicate and subject of the proposition. Therefore, it happens, as Boethius says (Hebdom., the title of which is: "Whether all that is, is good"), "that there are some mental concepts self-evident only to the learned, as that incorporeal substances are not in space." Therefore I say that this proposition, "God exists," of itself is self-evident, for the predicate is the same as the subject, because God is His own existence as will be hereafter shown (3, 4). Now because we do not know the essence of God, the proposition is not self-evident to us; but needs to be demonstrated by things that are more known to us, though less known in their nature — namely, by effects.

Reply to Objection 1. To know that God exists in a general and confused way is implanted in us by nature, inasmuch as God is man's beatitude. For man naturally desires happiness, and what is naturally desired by man must be naturally known to him. This, however, is not to know absolutely that God exists; just as to know that someone is approaching is not the same as to know that Peter is approaching, even though it is Peter who is approaching; for many there are who imagine that man's perfect good which is happiness, consists in riches, and others in pleasures, and others in something else.

Reply to Objection 2. Perhaps not everyone who hears this word "God" understands it to signify something than which nothing greater can be thought, seeing that some have believed God to be a body. Yet, granted that everyone understands that by this word "God" is signified something than which nothing greater can be thought, nevertheless, it does not therefore follow that he understands that what the word signifies exists actually, but only that it exists mentally. Nor can it be argued that it actually exists, unless it be admitted that there actually exists something than which nothing greater can be thought; and this precisely is not admitted by those who hold that God does not exist.

Reply to Objection 3. The existence of truth in general is self-evident but the existence of a Primal Truth is not self-evident to us.

Article 2. Whether it can be demonstrated that God exists?

<u>Objection 1.</u> It seems that the existence of God cannot be demonstrated. For it is an article of faith that God exists. But what is of faith cannot be demonstrated, because a demonstration produces scientific knowledge; whereas faith is of the unseen (Hebrews 11:1). Therefore it cannot be demonstrated that God exists.

<u>Objection 2.</u> Further, the essence is the middle term of demonstration. But we cannot know in what God's essence consists, but solely in what it does not consist; as Damascene says (De Fide Orth. i, 4). Therefore we cannot demonstrate that God exists.

<u>Objection 3.</u> Further, if the existence of God were demonstrated, this could only be from His effects. But His effects are not proportionate to Him, since He is infinite and His effects are finite; and between the finite and infinite there is no proportion. Therefore, since a cause cannot be demonstrated by an effect not proportionate to it, it seems that the existence of God cannot be demonstrated.

<u>On the contrary</u>, The Apostle says: "The invisible things of Him are clearly seen, being understood by the things that are made" (Romans 1:20). But this would not be unless the existence of God could be demonstrated through the things that are made; for the first thing we must know of anything is whether it exists.

<u>I answer that,</u> Demonstration can be made in two ways: One is through the cause, and is called "a priori," and this is to argue from what is prior absolutely. The other is through the

effect, and is called a demonstration "a posteriori"; this is to argue from what is prior relatively only to us. When an effect is better known to us than its cause, from the effect we proceed to the knowledge of the cause. And from every effect the existence of its proper cause can be demonstrated, so long as its effects are better known to us; because since every effect depends upon its cause, if the effect exists, the cause must pre-exist. Hence the existence of God, in so far as it is not self-evident to us, can be demonstrated from those of His effects which are known to us.

<u>Reply to Objection 1.</u> The existence of God and other like truths about God, which can be known by natural reason, are not articles of faith, but are preambles to the articles; for faith presupposes natural knowledge, even as grace presupposes nature, and perfection supposes something that can be perfected. Nevertheless, there is nothing to prevent a man, who cannot grasp a proof, accepting, as a matter of faith, something which in itself is capable of being scientifically known and demonstrated.

<u>Reply to Objection 2.</u> When the existence of a cause is demonstrated from an effect, this effect takes the place of the definition of the cause in proof of the cause's existence. This is especially the case in regard to God, because, in order to prove the existence of anything, it is necessary to accept as a middle term the meaning of the word, and not its essence, for the question of its essence follows on the question of its existence. Now the names given to God are derived from His effects; consequently, in demonstrating the existence of God from His effects, we may take for the middle term the meaning of the word "God".

Reply to Objection 3. From effects not proportionate to the cause no perfect knowledge of that cause can be obtained. Yet from every effect the existence of the cause can be clearly demonstrated, and so we can demonstrate the existence of God from His effects; though from them we cannot perfectly know God as He is in His essence.

Article 3. Whether God exists?

Objection 1. It seems that God does not exist; because if one of two contraries be infinite, the other would be altogether destroyed. But the word "God" means that He is infinite goodness. If, therefore, God existed, there would be no evil discoverable; but there is evil in the world. Therefore God does not exist.

Objection 2. Further, it is superfluous to suppose that what can be accounted for by a few principles has been produced by many. But it seems that everything we see in the world can be accounted for by other principles, supposing God did not exist. For all natural things can be reduced to one principle which is nature; and all voluntary things can be reduced to one principle which is human reason, or will. Therefore there is no need to suppose God's existence.

On the contrary, It is said in the person of God: "I am Who am." (Exodus 3:14)

I answer that, The existence of God can be proved in five ways.

The first and more manifest way is the argument from motion. It is certain, and evident to our senses, that in the world some things are in motion. Now whatever is in motion is put in motion by another, for nothing can be in motion except it is in potentiality to that towards which it is in motion; whereas a thing moves inasmuch as it is in act. For motion is nothing else than the reduction of something from potentiality to actuality. But nothing can be reduced from potentiality to actuality, except by something in a state of actuality. Thus that which is actually hot, as fire, makes wood, which is potentially hot, to be actually hot, and thereby moves and changes it. Now it is not possible that the same thing should be at once in actuality and potentiality in the same respect, but only in different respects. For what is actually hot cannot simultaneously be potentially hot; but it is simultaneously potentially cold. It is therefore impossible that in the same respect and in the same way a thing should be both mover and moved, i.e. that it should move itself. Therefore, whatever is in motion must be put in motion by another. If that by which it is put in motion be itself put in motion, then this also must needs be put in motion by another, and that by another again. But this cannot go on to infinity, because then there would be no first mover, and, consequently, no other mover; seeing that subsequent movers move only inasmuch as they are put in motion by the first mover; as the staff moves only because it is put in motion by the hand. Therefore it is necessary to arrive at a first mover, put in motion by no other; and this everyone understands to be God.

The second way is from the nature of the efficient cause. In the world of sense we find there is an order of efficient causes. There is no case known (neither is it, indeed, possible) in which a thing is found to be the efficient cause of itself; for so it would be prior to itself, which is impossible.

Now in efficient causes it is not possible to go on to infinity, because in all efficient causes following in order, the first is the cause of the intermediate cause, and the intermediate is the cause of the ultimate cause, whether the intermediate cause be several, or only one. Now to take away the cause is to take away the effect. Therefore, if there be no first cause among efficient causes, there will be no ultimate, nor any intermediate cause. But if in efficient causes it is possible to go on to infinity, there will be no first efficient cause, neither will there be an ultimate effect, nor any intermediate efficient causes; all of which is plainly false. Therefore it is necessary to admit a first efficient cause, to which everyone gives the name of God.

The third way is taken from possibility and necessity, and runs thus. We find in nature things that are possible to be and not to be, since they are found to be generated, and to corrupt, and consequently, they are possible to be and not to be. But it is impossible for these always to exist, for that which is possible not to be at some time is not. Therefore, if everything is possible not to be, then at one time there could have been nothing in existence. Now if this were true, even now there would be nothing in existence, because that which does not exist only begins to exist by something already existing. Therefore, if at one time nothing was in existence, it would have been impossible for anything to have begun to exist; and thus even now nothing would be in existence — which is absurd. Therefore, not all beings are merely possible, but there must exist something the existence of which is necessary. But every necessary thing either has its necessity caused by another, or not. Now it is impossible to go on to infinity in necessary things which have their necessity caused by another, as has been already proved in regard to efficient causes. Therefore we cannot but postulate the existence of some being having of itself its own necessity, and not receiving it from another, but rather causing in others their necessity. This all men speak of as God.

The fourth way is taken from the gradation to be found in things. Among beings there are some more and some less good, true, noble and the like. But "more" and "less" are predicated of different things, according as they resemble in their different ways something which is the maximum, as a thing is said to be hotter according as it more nearly resembles that which is hottest; so that there is something which is truest, something best, something noblest and, consequently, something which is uttermost being; for those things that are greatest in truth are greatest in being, as it is written in Metaph. ii. Now the maximum in any genus is the cause of all in that genus; as fire, which is the maximum heat, is the cause of all hot things. Therefore there must also be something which is to all beings the cause of their being, goodness, and every other perfection; and this we call God.

The fifth way is taken from the governance of the world. We see that things which lack intelligence, such as natural bodies, act for an end, and this is evident from their acting always, or nearly always, in the same way, so as to obtain the best result. Hence it is plain that not fortuitously, but designedly, do they achieve their end. Now whatever lacks intelligence cannot move towards an end, unless it be directed by some being endowed with knowledge and intelligence; as the arrow is shot to its mark by the archer. Therefore some intelligent being exists by whom all natural things are directed to their end; and this being we call God.

Reply to Objection 1. As Augustine says (Enchiridion xi): "Since God is the highest good, He would not allow any evil to exist in His works, unless His omnipotence and goodness were such as to bring good even out of evil." This is part of the infinite goodness of God, that He should allow evil to exist, and out of it produce good.

Reply to Objection 2. Since nature works for a determinate end under the direction of a higher agent, whatever is done by nature must needs be traced back to God, as to its first cause. So also whatever is done voluntarily must also be traced back to some higher cause other than human reason or will, since these can change or fail; for all things that are changeable and capable of defect must be traced back to an immovable and self-necessary first principle, as was shown in the body of the Article.